The Art of
HOLDING

—

The Art of
HOLDING

PRINCIPLES & TECHNIQUES

MARC TEDESCHI

Weatherhill

The Art of Holding: Principles & Techniques

Copyright © 2001 by Marc Tedeschi

Published by Weatherhill Inc., 41 Monroe Turnpike,
Trumbull, CT 06611 USA. Protected by copyright
under the terms of the International Copyright
Union; all rights reserved. Except for fair use in
book reviews, no part of this book may be used or
reproduced for any reason by any means, including
any method of photographic or electronic repro-
duction, without permission. Printed in China on
acid-free paper meeting the ANSI Z39.48 Standard.

FIRST EDITION, 2001
First Printing

Book and cover design: Marc Tedeschi
Photography: Shelley Firth, Frank Deras
Creative consultant: Michele Wetherbee
Editorial supervision: Ray Furse, Thomas Tedeschi
Printing and binding: Oceanic Graphic Printing
and C&C Offset Printing in China
Typeset in Helvetica Neue, Univers, Sabon,
Adobe Garamond, Weiss, and Times.

Library of Congress Cataloging-in-Publication Data
Tedeschi, Marc.
   The art of holding: principles & techniques /
Marc Tedeschi.—1st ed.
      p. cm.
   Includes bibliographical references.
   ISBN 0-8348-0491-3
   1. Martial arts—Holding. I. Title
GV1102.7.H64 .T43 2001
796.8—dc21   2001026247

Trademarks:
Kuk Sool Won™ and Hwa Rang Do® are claimed
as trademarks of their respective owners.

—

*For Professor Wally Jay,
a generous and innovative teacher,
who helped me to perceive the
common threads that run
through all martial arts.*

—

CONTENTS

Editorial Notes
The information in this book is a reorganized and expanded version of material found in the author's 1136-page *Hapkido*, and employs similar editorial conventions: To avoid sexist grammar, *they, them, their,* and *themselves* are used in place of the singular pronouns *he, she, him, her, his, hers, himself,* and *herself*. To avoid wordiness, articles may be omitted, and abbreviations are employed: (R) for right, (L) for left.

This book outlines the essential principles and techniques that define the art of holding in most martial arts. The technical differences between most martial styles are defined by the unique ways in which they use and combine skills. This is largely determined by philosophical ideas, as the techniques themselves are often very similar. The reasons for this are not difficult to grasp: since all martial techniques seek to capitalize on strengths and limitations of the human form, they by necessity come to similar conclusions and embody similar

OVERVIEW

technical principles. While these principles may be expressed differently in different styles, they usually reflect the same basic concepts. The techniques in this book come from Hapkido, a varied and practical martial art that shares historical and technical similarities with many other arts, such as Aki-Jujutsu, Jujutsu, Aikido, Judo, Chinese Chin Na, Kuk Sool Won, and Hwa Rang Do. It is hoped this book will enrich your practice, regardless of style, and help you to recognize your style's place within the larger culture of martial arts.

Introduction

Holding techniques are used to *seize and control* an opponent so that their movement is restricted—thus hindering or eliminating their ability to continue fighting. Holds are characterized by grabbing, squeezing, pressing, twisting, bending, leveraging, breaking, or strangulation attacks, which are directed to joints, muscles, tendons, ligaments, bones, pressure points, and blood vessels. Holding techniques are commonly used to cause pain, limit motor functions, or restrict the flow of air or blood to the brain. In comprehensive self-defense arts, such as Hapkido, holds are used offensively or defensively from standing or ground postures, often in combination with other strikes, blocks, or throws.

The material in this book will cover basic principles, fundamental skills, common holds, combination holds and transitions, and defenses against joint locks—all of the categories that typically define the art of holding. Most of the techniques in this book are shown in the context of self-defense; however, sport-oriented martial arts will often embody similar principles. In eclectic martial arts, such as Hapkido, *holding* is never thought of as an isolated body of techniques, but rather as an integral part of a larger system embracing a broad range of martial skills (strikes, blocks, holds, throws, etc.). Those martial artists seeking an eclectic, comprehensive approach to self-defense, should obtain the author's 1136-page book, *Hapkido: Traditions, Philosophy, Technique.*

Historical Development

The act of grabbing and restraining an attacker's arm or weapon is a very natural and instinctive method of defense, and probably among the oldest forms of unarmed fighting. The specific origin of holds is not known, although they are thought to have evolved concurrently in different geographic regions, along with other forms of combat. Some of the earliest recorded use of seizing arts occurred in China, where these skills are collectively referred to as *Chin Na* (meaning to seize and control). Chin Na techniques

evolved over a period of thousands of years, and were mostly practiced in secret by the military. Around AD 500, the politically active Shaolin temple began to become extensively involved in developing and practicing these arts, although they would not be disseminated into the general population until around the 19th century. Some historians believe that the spread of Chin Na into neighboring regions influenced development of native Korean and Japanese arts. Other historians hypothesize that all these regions developed their own native martial systems, and subsequently influenced one another to varying degrees.

In the martial arts world today, the art of *seizing and controlling* can be found in almost all styles, although the level of sophistication and range of technique varies widely. Nonetheless, one finds an amazing similarity when observing the basic biomechanical principles at work. In fact there are many basic wrist locks that can be found in virtually all martial arts. This is not surprising, since the common denominator is the human body. Whether you live in Asia, Europe, or the Americas, your joints bend freely one way and not in another. Since all humans possess the same anatomical construction, methods of attacking the body's weaknesses are essentially the same. The fundamental differences between the holding techniques of various martial arts has more to do with matters of philosophy, application theory, and technique preference. The idea that a specific hold is unique to one martial art exclusively is naive and can only come from limited exposure to other arts.

Today, most contemporary improvements in holding techniques have resulted from either sport competition or the pioneering efforts of individuals. Most innovation-oriented martial arts continue to influence each other. When comparing older holding methods with more modern innovations, one notices greater biomechanical efficiency and increased speed of execution. The use of pressure points in holds is also becoming more commonplace as Asian traditions of secrecy rapidly dissolve in a blitz of books, videos, and seminars.

Types of Holds

This book documents 112 common holds, which can be varied in almost limitless ways depending upon the attack, methods of entry, specific grips, delivery motion, supporting body movement, and footwork. Consequently, when studying with different teachers, one is likely to observe different ways of executing the same technique. While variations are endless, basic principles remain the same. Generally, holds are made up of complex motions that can be circular, linear, or totally irregular. Holds used in martial arts generally fall into the following categories:

- Joint Holds
- Choke Holds
- Nerve Holds
- Pinning Holds

Joint Holds

If you limit joint movement, you reduce an opponent's ability to move. Joint holds (also called joint locks) force a joint to move in an abnormal direction, which can be potentially destructive. The level of force determines the degree of damage. This may involve extreme pain, tearing of muscles, tearing tendons from their connections to muscle or bone, tearing ligaments from their connections between bones (dislocation), or breaking the bone itself (fracture). In most situations, it is not necessary to damage the joint, since pain alone will deter many attacks and secure most holds. However, in certain situations, breaking or dislocating the joint may be required to ensure your safety. For instance, if your life is threatened, an attacker is not deterred by pain, or you are engaging multiple attackers and must dispense with one to quickly address the others. *Breaking a joint* essentially renders that limb useless and causes intense pain that may cause the attacker to faint. Although individuals under the influence of powerful narcotics may not feel pain, a broken joint remains inoperable.

The most common joint holds involve attacks to the wrist, elbow, and shoulder, and secondarily, to the fingers, toes, ankle, knee, hip, and spine. Joint holds are used to restrain movement, assist a throw, direct an opponent into a harmful obstacle (e.g., a wall or door), direct an opponent into a more secure position (e.g., a better hold), or escort a person from one location to another. Joint holds are effective because they: 1) cause pain, or 2) damage the joint, limiting mobility.

Choke Holds

Choke holds are used to reduce or eliminate the flow of blood or air to the brain by strangulation, often resulting in loss of consciousness or death. This usually involves clamping holds to the carotid artery, jugular vein, and vagus nerve at the side of the neck (which restricts blood flow); or to the windpipe at the front of the neck (which restricts air flow). Chokes can also involve painful pressure to nerves on the neck. Choke holds are commonly applied using the hands and arms, although chokes using the legs and feet are also possible. Choke holds are often used to render an opponent unconscious, assist throws, or weaken an attacker during grappling. Choke holds to blood vessels are considered safer, since an attacker can usually be revived. Choke holds to the windpipe are *not safe,* since damage may require immediate surgery to prevent loss of life.

Nerve Holds

Nerve holds use grabbing, pressing, squeezing, and gouging actions to attack sensitive points. Nerve holds are often used with, or are a part of, joint holds or chokes. They are used to cause pain, control movement, impair motor functions, reduce Ki-flow (weakening an attacker), or produce unconsciousness. The effect depends upon the point targeted, the degree of accuracy, and other principles.

Pinning Holds

Pinning holds are used to restrain movement by pinning an opponent to the ground, or against a wall or other obstacle. Pinning holds can consist of joint holds or chokes, or may simply involve the use of your body weight. Pins are usually integrated with other techniques, and are included in most chapters.

Responsible Use of Force

Martial techniques such as holds should only be used for self-defense, the protection of others, physical exercise, or in organized sport competition between consenting individuals. The use of force to resolve a situation carries with it a social and moral responsibility to apply force in an appropriate and sensible manner. When we attempt to control another person by striking, holding, or throwing, our expertise in martial arts and our knowledge of the human body allows us not only to attack with increased efficiency, but with greater compassion. By manipulating the body's weak points and using skillful, efficient techniques, it becomes possible to immobilize or restrain an attacker without causing serious or permanent injury. Our degree of skill directly influences our ability to do this safely, without endangering ourselves. To seriously injure or kill someone is not very difficult. It requires no special knowledge, and often occurs unintentionally. For the skilled martial artist, the *excessive use of force* is an inexcusable and morally reprehensible act, deserving condemnation.

Types of Holds

Joint Hold

Joint Hold (leg lock used to initiate throw)

Choke Hold

Nerve Hold

Pinning Hold (while standing)

Pinning Hold (while ground fighting)

Comparing Martial Arts

The photos on the following four pages show examples of similar holds from different martial arts, as they are applied by notable masters. In some cases, the differences are obvious; others require a more educated eye or prior experience with specific styles to be able to perceive the subtle distinctions that distinguish one art from another.

The purpose of these photos is not to make any particular point, but to invite the reader to look outside of their own art. Understanding how other martial arts interpret similar techniques can lead one to a deeper understanding of their own art, and its place in the larger culture of martial arts. Please recognize that these photos have been selected for their similarities. Each of these martial

arts also possess numerous qualities and techniques that are relatively unique unto themselves. Please to do not assume that by looking at these photos you understand these arts. To make in depth comparisons and draw intelligent conclusions would require the examination of hundreds of techniques, decades of training, and a great deal of familiarity with specific martial arts.

Hapkido: Elbow Arm Bar as demonstrated by the author in his book Hapkido: Traditions, Philosophy, Technique

Judo: Kataude Dori (defense against "Single-Hand Hold," from the Kodokan Goshin Jutsu kata), as demonstrated in the book Kodokan Judo by Judo founder Jigoro Kano, 1956

Jujutsu: Elbow arm bar as demonstrated by Grandmaster Wally Jay in his book Small Circle Jujutsu, 1989

Aikido: *Ikkyo (The First Movement) as demonstrated by Kisshomaru Ueshiba in his book,* Aikido, *1985*

Tai Chi Chuan: *Lao Han Bai Jiang (An Old Man Visits the General) as demonstrated by Jwing-Ming Yang in his book* Taiji Chin Na, *1995*

Kuk Sool Won: *Arm bar as demonstrated by He-Young Kimm in his book* Kuk Sool: Korean Martial Arts, *1985*

Hwa Rang Do: *Elbow Break as demonstrated by Hwa Rang Do founder Lee-Joo Bang in his book* The Ancient Martial Art of Hwa Rang Do: Vol. 2, *1979*

Hapkido: Outward Wrist Lock as demonstrated by the author in his book Hapkido: Traditions, Philosophy, Technique

Aiki-Jujutsu: Kote Gaeshi (Wrist Twist) as demonstrated by Shiro Omiya in his book The Hidden Roots of Aikido: Aiki Jujutsu Daitoryu, *1992*

Jujutsu: Twisting wrist lock as demonstrated by Grandmaster Wally Jay in his book Small Circle Jujutsu, *1989*

Aikido: A portion of Kote Gaeshi (Wrist Twist) against a punch, as demonstrated by Mitsugi Saotome in his book The Principles of Aikido, *1989*

Hapkido: Passing Shoulder Lock as demonstrated by the author in his book Hapkido: Traditions, Philosophy, Technique

Hwa Rang Do: Shoulder Break Throw as demonstrated by Hwa Rang Do founder Lee-Joo Bang in his book The Ancient Martial Art of Hwa Rang Do: Vol. 2, 1979

Aikido: Shiho Nage (Four-Corner Throw) as demonstrated by Aikido founder Morihei Ueshiba in his book Budo, 1938

Judo: Ude Garami (Entangled Arm Lock) as demonstrated in the book Judo: Formal Techniques by Tadao Otaki and Donn Draeger, 1983

When building a house, one begins with the foundation. If the foundation is strong, the building's structure will be able to withstand the trials of nature and time. If the foundation is weak, the entire structure will be undermined, and its life span more limited. Before learning and practicing specific martial holds, it is important to first understand the basic principles that govern the execution of virtually all holding techniques. A proper grasp of fundamentals and basic skills will allow practitioners to learn more quickly, refine their

FUNDAMENTALS

skills to a higher degree, enjoy their training, and avoid the unnecessary injuries commonly resulting from improperly applied holds and unskilled methods of falling. The process of learning to apply holds should not be painful or injurious, but rather a gradual, confidence-building experience that leaves one exhilarated and looking forward to more training. This chapter will outline basic principles and techniques, all of which must be learned from a qualified instructor to ensure that your martial training is safe and rewarding.

Ki

The word *Ki* (also written as *Qi*, *Chi*, or *Gi*) is essentially untranslatable, although it is often described as the "vital energy" or "life force" that permeates the universe, flowing through and animating all things. It has been the basis of Oriental medicine for thousands of years.

In martial arts, the combative use of Ki usually involves blending and harmonizing your own Ki (internal energy) with that of your opponent and the greater universe. This is done to assist the application of a technique, such as a strike, hold, throw, or escape. Although skillful technique does not require Ki manipulation to be highly effective, focusing Ki will increase a technique's efficiency. When fighting a highly skilled or overpowering opponent, harmonized Ki may be the difference between a technique that works and one that fails. In energy-oriented martial arts, such as Hapkido, Aikido, and Tai Chi Chuan, one's ability to strengthen and control Ki is developed through exercises and meditation. For serious practitioners trying to develop their Ki, a variety of factors must be in balance—diet, air quality, emotional state, sleep, sexual activity, and the level of stress in your life all affect the levels of Ki in your body.

Live-Hand

The term *Live-Hand* refers to specific hand formations which are used in the martial art Hapkido to increase the flow of Ki into the hands and arms. This increases arm strength and power when most needed, such as during a wrist escape or the application of a hold.

Live-Hand techniques involve visualization, breath control, and tensing of the fingers, hands, and arms. Concentration and focus are very important, as is practice. The use of a Live-Hand is typically characterized by extending one or more fingers and breathing out as a specific technique is applied.

As previously stated, the techniques in this book come from Hapkido; thus, one will notice the use of Live-Hands in many techniques. If you practice a martial art that does not use Live-Hands, merely ignore that portion of the technique. Live-Hands are not a crucial component of the holds shown, but rather one of the useful additions that can create greater efficiency.

In recent years, the use of extended fingers in combat has fallen into disfavor among some practitioners due to their increased vulnerability to attack or damage. Today many stylists restrict Live-Hand use in fighting to wrist escapes, well-controlled breaking blocks, or holds in which the extra power is often needed and the fingers are well-protected from being grabbed or broken.

Typical Live-Hand Formations

The photographs shown below illustrate two typical Live-Hand formations. In the lower-left photographs, a basic Live-Hand is formed by spreading all five fingers very wide, with the thumb slightly bent. This hand formation expands and hardens the wrist and forearm, concentrating Ki in the hand and fingertips.

It is often used to apply wrist escapes, blocks, and arm bars. In the lower-right photographs, a Live-Hand is formed by closing the hand, with only the forefinger extended (in some techniques, the thumb is also extended). This formation is often used when gripping an attacker's fingers, wrist, arm, or ankle.

Breath Control

Proper breathing when executing techniques is essential. Do not hold your breath. During training or combat, try to breathe deeply and rhythmically. This calms the mind, oxygenates the blood, and maximizes the flow of Ki throughout the body, encouraging peak performance. In most martial arts, you will exhale as a technique is applied or a hold is executed. This helps coordinate physical actions, increases physical strength, and channels Ki to the extremities; it is is often referred to as *breath power* or *extending one's Ki*. Conceptually, three actions (breathing, physical action, and the flow of Ki from one's center to the limbs) become one coordinated, powerful response. When these actions are intimately linked to an opponent's energies and actions, technique becomes effortless.

The Energy-Shout

The distinct shout many martial artists emit when executing techniques is essentially breathing meditation converted to dynamic action. In Korean, this energy harmonizing shout is referred to as a *Kihap*. In the Japanese language it is called a *Kiai*. Most Chinese arts do not use an audible shout.

Live-Hand with five fingers spread (locking attacker's elbow to immobilize them)

Live-Hand with forefinger extended (locking attacker's finger to immobilize them)

The word *Ki* is defined as the universal energy or dynamic force that animates all things. *Hap* or *Ai* is the root form for words which connote harmonizing, coming together, or coordinating. Thus the concept of *Kihap* or *Kiai* literally means to harmonize with the dynamic universal life force. The "energy-harmonizing shout" is a means, then, of coordinating our actions with the flow of energies and events of which we are part. All individual actions and events merge into a single flow. This is what is meant by "being at one with the universe."

The Dynamic Release of Energy
When you execute a punch, kick, hold, or throw, or block a strike, energy is released—typically as a rush of air from the lungs. This exhalation of air, coordinated with muscular tension in the body and throat, creates the deep, roaring growl of the true energy-shout. When you are first learning martial arts, the energy-shout will mostly be an artificial adornment, merely accompanying physical actions. However, if you train in an uninhibited way, focusing on the purpose of the shout, you will eventually develop a shout that is natural, spontaneous, and uninhibited. It will become a reflection of your dynamic emotional state, and an expression of the harmonized, total commitment of your body, mind, and spirit to the techniques you are executing. The true energy-shout is often characterized as a low, deep, harsh roar that emerges from the diaphragm, instead of the throat. It should be an expression of indomitable spirit, not fright.

The Silent Shout
The silent shout is not an audible shout, but rather a total commitment of body, mind, emotions, and spirit into the events of the moment. There is no thought of the outcome, only the now. You are completely in tune with your opponent's actions. The silent shout is considered to be the highest level of energy-harmonizing. If there is any sound at all, it might be characterized as a low humming "ohmm" sound, which is a reflection of your own breathing in unison with the events transpiring before you. Remember, the ultimate objective is not to make noise, but to develop a natural and effortless unification of body, mind, and spirit.

Leading and Blending
Leading refers to the act of directing your opponent into a strike, hold, or throw by using their own energy against them. This may involve redirecting a strike or charge, or creating an initially deceptive movement that causes your opponent to react by moving in a direction that assists the execution of your technique. Leading movements can be short or long depending on circumstances, and are often executed in the opposite direction in which you intend your opponent to move. For example, if you pull an opponent's arm toward your right, they will usually react by pulling to your left. This sets up specific techniques.

Blending refers to the act of uniting with your opponent's force. This reduces your chances of injury and increases the efficiency of your techniques, by avoiding a direct confrontation with your opponent's forces. Blending can be thought of metaphorically, as occupying the calm space within a tornado, or joining with the force of the tornado by matching its speed and motion. This is accomplished by knowing when to give way and when to attack. Blending is particularly important when countering with holds or throws, or facing an overpowering opponent. In practical terms, leading and blending require good footwork, timing, speed, power, and versatility, as demonstrated in the photo sequence below.

Pressure Point Attacks
Some martial arts, such as Hapkido, make extensive use of pressure points (also called *acupoints*) to assist the application of techniques, including holds. These are the same points commonly used in Eastern medicine to heal the human body. Manipulating pressure points alters the body's energetic state by affecting Ki-flow and neurological functions. In martial arts, specific pressure points may be struck or pressed to cause pain; reduce physical strength; cause involuntary muscle responses; limit motor functions; cause loss of consciousness; or damage neurological, respiratory, or circulatory functions. In holding techniques, pressure point attacks are mostly used to assist your entry, keep an opponent from countering, or reduce an opponent's strength. In this book, pressure points are cited using their standard alphanumeric name (e.g., TW-11). Common points are shown at the end of this chapter.

Leading, blending, breath control, and complete harmony with an attacker's energy are demonstrated in a "one-hand" joint lock hold.

HOLDING PRINCIPLES

The following seventeen basic principles are essential to the proper execution of most holding techniques. These concepts are common to many martial arts, and continue to be refined as new developments occur.

1. Grab and Stick

Before you can apply any holding technique, you must first secure an opponent's limb by remaining in constant contact (sticking) as you enter into the hold. This requires a certain degree of sensitivity in being able to feel or sense your opponent's movement as you lead them into a hold or series of holds. Grabbing a punch is easier said than done, and is extremely difficult even against a slower fighter. Grabbing blocks, trapping parries, and jamming the attack before it is launched are common methods of securing a grip. You can also surprise an opponent by grabbing while they are stationary or pausing, or when they are already holding you.

Grabbing a Punch
Generally, there are three moments when it is desirable to attempt grabbing an opponent's arm to enter a hold:

- Grab during a pause (1.1)
- Grab when the punch is extended (1.2)
- Strike, then grab as an attacker blocks (1.3)

2. Lead into a Hold

Leading refers to the act of directing your opponent into a hold by using their own energy against them. Basic concepts were covered previously under *Energetic Concepts*. Leading movements can be short or long depending on circumstances, and are often executed in the opposite direction in which you intend your opponent to move. For example, if you pull an opponent's arm toward your right, they will usually react by pulling to your left, setting up specific holds (see photo 2.2).

Long Leading vs. Short Leading
This is often a source of controversy and confusion for many martial artists, who often believe that one method is superior to the other. Whether you use long, pronounced leading or short, quick leading, is a function of *what you are trying to accomplish.* It is not a question of "short leading is better than long leading" or vice versa. Do what is best for a given situation. For example, in static situations against a quick opponent, long slow movements are easily countered. In these situations, use short leading to apply the hold more quickly. In situations where you need to initiate motion or keep attackers moving, long leading motions can accelerate their motions, generate confusion, and lead them into awkward or unbalanced postures.

3. Blend with Attacker's Force

This basic concept was covered previously under *Energetic Concepts*. Blending footwork and body turns are all important elements. When applying holds, never directly oppose your opponent's strength. Use their strength against them by employing leading principles.

1.1 Grab during a pause (grabbing the arm while it is stationary, between strikes)

1.2 Parry and grab (parrying and leading a punch as you grab the wrist)

1.3 Strike and grab (executing a punch to draw opponent's block, then grabbing their arm as you retract)

2.1 Lead into a Hold (using pronounced leading to generate movement and redirect a charging attacker into a wrist hold)

2.2 Lead into a Hold (using short leading to quickly enter a hold; same wrist hold as above)

3. Blend with Attacker's Force

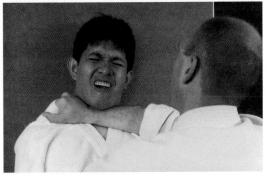

4. Eliminate Space and Play (Left: using chest, arms, and knee to apply arm bar. Right: using wall to assist a choke)

If your opponent resists a hold, negating its effect, immediately make a transition to another hold using the path of least resistance. Never oppose force, unless you are clearly stronger. Meeting force with force can lead to unnecessary injuries, to you as well as to your opponent.

4. Eliminate Space and Play

When applying holds, particularly joint locks and chokes, it is very important to eliminate extra space. Any *looseness* or *free-play* in the hold will diminish its effectiveness and encourage escapes or counters. When gripping, clamping, or wrapping, make sure that your limbs or body are tight against the surfaces you are holding. Joints should be locked tight before applying pressure, as this provides a more direct transfer of energy. You can also use other parts of your body or the environment to prevent excess movement. For example, use the wall or ground to stabilize the neck when applying a one-arm choke, or your palm or chest to secure finger locks and wrist locks.

5. Apply Complex Force

Many martial holds, particularly joint locks, use complex motions that apply force in several directions at once. Depending on the hold, this is often characterized as bending and twisting, pushing and pulling, or turning and lifting. Applying complex force puts greater stress on a joint, thereby reducing the level of force needed to create pain or damage the joint. Complex force can also transfer additional stress to related joints. For example, an *Elevated Wrist Lock* (see 5.2) primarily stresses the joints of the fingers and wrist, and secondarily the elbow and shoulder. When a hold stresses several joints at once, it becomes more efficient, more painful, and can create more widespread damage.

6. Use Purposeful Movement

Any footwork or body movement that accompanies a hold should serve a purpose, otherwise it is extraneous. Movement is used to place yourself in an optimal position to: reduce the level of force needed to make a hold work, reduce counterattack options, or occupy safer space. Generally, when applying holds you are strongest when your arms are closer to your trunk, and weaker if they are extended or raised above the shoulders. For this reason, it is common to either pull your opponent in toward your body, or to step inward. Motions that lead an attacker, redirect energy, or apply force should be as simple and direct as possible. Always look for ways to simplify your movements.

7. Be Biomechanically Efficient

All holds, particularly joint locks, attempt to capitalize on basic anatomical weaknesses in the human body. The movements used when applying a hold should contribute to exploiting these weaknesses. Any movement that does not is essentially wasted energy. Some holding techniques require speed, timing, and dexterity, while others rely more on strength. The holds that work best are those which are quick, short, simple, and precise, and do not rely on excessive force. Practice gently, so you can judge the efficiency of your skills. Using excess force only hides your mistakes.

5.1 Apply Complex Force (Bent Wrist Lock)

5.2 Apply Complex Force (wrist lock with finger hold)

6.1 Use Purposeful Movement (stepping inward and across to cut off counterstrikes and unbalance attacker)

6.2 Use Purposeful Movement (stepping backward to assist a wrist lock, unbalance attacker, and move away)

8.1 Focus Energy (circular force focused at joint)

8.2 Focus Energy (linear force focused at nerve)

When comparing the technique of a novice with that of an expert, the differences are quite obvious. Novices tend to use excessive and extraneous motions, too much muscle power, and often lack focus when finishing the hold. As they improve, their motions will become briefer, more flowing, and less muscular. They will also be able to *feel* the hold as it is applied, using only enough force to control the opponent without seriously hurting them. As further expertise is gained, they will modify and improvise on the basic motions, *customizing* the technique in response to the changing dynamics of a fight. They will begin to use the power of their entire body to apply the hold. This does not mean *more power,* but rather, more *controlled* power with less effort. Economical technique usually develops more quickly in smaller individuals, since they cannot rely on their strength. Regardless of your size, obtaining a high level of proficiency requires an excellent teacher.

Circular Movement

The traditional concept of circular movement has been discussed at length throughout this book. When applying holds, *circles* are often used as a metaphor to describe the motion used to apply a specific hold—particularly joint holds. While this serves as a useful shorthand for novices attempting to master the intricacies of complex movements, it is sometimes a gross simplification of the actual forces at work. In reality many holding techniques use a complex combination of movements, which can be linear, circular, or even totally irregular. Holding techniques are made more efficient by concentrating on the natural weakness of a joint, rather than on abstract ideals of geometric perfection. If you understand these weaknesses, you will understand why a technique works and why it does not, and will better understand the type of force that must be applied. Observation and anatomical knowledge are essential.

8. Focus Energy

When executing holds, try to focus energy at very specific points. To focus energy *physically* requires nothing more than good, efficient technique which transmits force to the smallest possible area—usually a nerve, tendon, or acupoint. To focus energy *mentally* requires visualization and total concentration. This is characterized by *seeing* the intended result in your mind. This same principle is also used to resist a hold. For example, as an attacker applies a wrist lock, visualize your hand spinning in the opposite direction of their force. You will find pain is reduced and your ability to resist increases. *Focusing energy* can also involve projecting destructive Ki into your opponent or bleeding Ki from them. This requires years of training, emotional maturity, and the guidance of a gifted individual. More basic Ki manipulation is accomplished by using acupoints and specific hand formations to weaken an attacker's resistance.

7.1 Be Biomechanically Efficient (wrist lock applied using short economical movements as attacker grabs)

7.2 Same hold as above except: Excess motion slows entry, encouraging escape (arm raised too high, insufficient body rotation, hand not trapped tight, body not supporting hold)

9. Use Ki-Power

Ki-power refers to the use of *Ki* (internal energy) and *adrenaline* (a hormone released by the adrenal glands) to assist the application of a technique, such as a hold. While *Ki-power* is a fundamental principle incorporated into all techniques found in energy-based martial arts, such as Hapkido, nowhere is it more important and clearly evident than in holding arts. Although skillful technique does not require the use of Ki-power to be highly effective, focusing Ki will increase a hold's efficiency by increasing one's physical and mental power. This can be essential against overpowering opponents who negate your skill with superior strength, weight, and speed. The use of Ki-power can also help compensate for technical errors that inevitably occur when executing holds in highly stressful situations, such as combat.

When executing holds or escapes, the use of Ki-power is often characterized by extending one or more fingers in a Live-Hand formation and breathing out as the technique is applied. Sometimes the martial artist will also emit an energy-harmonizing shout to coordinate and focus one's power. These ideas were outlined previously, at the start of this chapter, under *Energetic Concepts*.

10. Modulate Force

Varying the amount of force, or the direction of your attack, can be used to reduce an opponent's resistance to a technique. For example, when applying joint locks, momentarily relax the hold, then apply leverage forcefully (repeat the motion as needed). Shaking the joint, or making small, jerky, abrupt motions while applying a hold is also effective. Radical changes in direction can assist a hold by unbalancing an opponent, and by redirecting your energy in a direction that the opponent is unprepared to resist.

11. Use Acupoints and Nerves

The use of sensitive acupoints or nerves (typically called *pressure points*) greatly increases a technique's efficiency by creating pain, limiting mobility, weakening musculature, or producing unconsciousness. Many of the holds shown in this book involve simultaneous attacks to specific acupoints—often in combination with strikes or pressing attacks. The use of acupoints or nerves is not mandatory, but can definitely increase your chances of success. The underlying medical principles, on which these attacks are based, are outlined in the author's book, *Essential Anatomy for Healing and Martial Arts*.

12. Distract and Deceive

Executing a variable, unpredictable, irregular attack is an important principle adopted by many martial arts. This concept can also be applied to holding techniques to make counters and escapes more difficult. Feints should be used to intentionally mislead your opponent as to your real intentions. For example, reach for one hand, and grab the other. Strikes can also be used to lower an opponent's resistance to a hold, by dividing their attention and forcing them to worry about other threats. A typical example involves striking or shouting to distract an opponent as you apply the hold. *Distraction* can also involve manipulating an attacker's auto-responses by tricking their body. This usually involves striking or pressing motor-nerves, which causes muscles to momentarily relax, allowing you to apply the hold. Remember, anytime you break your opponent's concentration, you will negatively affect that person's timing, strength, and ability to resist the hold.

13. Operate from a Superior Position

When executing holds, try to place your body in positions where you are strongest and your opponent is weakest. When you occupy a superior position, your physical strength and balance is optimized, and your posture makes counterattacks more difficult. This often involves stepping inward or crowding, while leading the opponent's limbs into the most efficient positions. Maintain a strong balance while you work to unbalance your attacker. This is called *destroying one's root*. Once the balance is compromised, it will be more difficult for an opponent to resist or counter (but not impossible). Do not over-lean or use excessive footwork. Try to make your opponent do most of the work. All of the basic principles discussed in this section contribute to maintaining a superior position.

Live-Hand Pros+Cons

Historically, Live-Hands were used in many holds to increase strength and generate Ki-power. Today many practitioners refrain from using them in certain holds, since they are vulnerable to finger locks (A–B). When your hands are well protected from grabs, Live-Hands can be used quite safely (C). It is also important to remember that in some arts such as Hapkido, most holds are applied with great speed, immobilizing an opponent very quickly. Thus, it is unlikely your opponent will possess the time or reflexes to grab your fingers during the brief moment they are vulnerable.

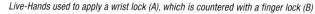

Live-Hands used to apply a wrist lock (A), which is countered with a finger lock (B)   *Live-Hands used in a protected position*

A Apply Force Upward

B Opponent Counters by Bending Arm

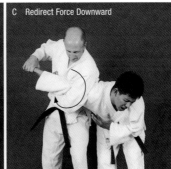
C Redirect Force Downward

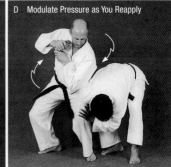
D Modulate Pressure as You Reapply

10. *Modulate Force (redirecting an "arm bar" and modulating pressure to overcome a strong opponent)*

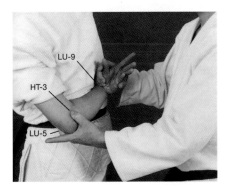

LU-9

HT-3

LU-5

11.1 Use Acupoints (pressing to assist a joint hold)

N-UE-19a
M-UE-24
M-UE-50
TW-3

11.2 Use Acupoints (raking the hand to escape a grab)

TW-17

11.3 Use Acupoints (pressing to assist a choke entry)

A

B

C

12. *Distract and Deceive (poke to the eyes releases a choke and distracts an attacker from the wrist lock being applied; a Shin Kick creates further distraction)*

A

B

13.1 Operate from a Superior Position (strong position allows a joint hold to transition to a ground pin)

13.2 Weak Position (hand too high, too far from body)

14. Transition within the Flow of Combat

Real combat is rarely decided on the basis of a single technique. The ability to make transitions from one hold to another is crucial, as is the ability to recognize these opportunities during the flow of combat, which is constantly changing. For every technique, there is a counter; and for every counter, another counter. The more skillful your opponents are, the more easily they will move to negate your attack or defense.

When executing a hold, always be ready to make a transition at any time into other holds, strikes, or throws as circumstances dictate. When making a transition between holds, maintain pressure and control throughout the change. The hallmark of any masterful martial artist is that person's ability to make smooth, effortless transitions from one technique to another, constantly adjusting to the opponent's rhythm, balance, and power.

If you are truly in sync with your opponent's movements, transitions should require very little effort. Sensitivity, feeling, and economy of motion are the most important qualities to cultivate. Strength is mostly irrelevant.

If you are confronting an opponent who negates your counters and transitions with superior skill or power, try switching your attack to a totally different part of the body. If an opponent's attention is focused on protecting the joints of one arm, then they will likely be unprepared for an attack to another area, such as the head, legs, or other arm. The key to successful transitions is to anticipate, and to move just slightly ahead of your opponent. When your opponent gets ahead of you, you will be vulnerable to counters. When you are *being controlled* by skilled transition artists, accelerate your movements ahead of theirs. This will provide the space you need to apply a counter and seize the advantage.

Explanation for Sequence 14.1

A–B. Attacker grabs defender's wrist. Defender uses a Wrist Escape and Shoulder Butt, to set up a *Bent-Arm Wrist Lock.*

C–D. Attacker counters by straightening his arm. Defender transitions to a *Forearm Arm Bar.*

E–F. Attacker counters with a Shoulder Roll. Defender transitions to an *Outward Wrist Lock.*

G–H. Attacker counters by rolling sideways. Defender transitions to a *Finger Lock,* which he uses to pin the opponent.

Explanation for Sequence 14.2

A–B. Defender escapes a choke and transitions to an *Elevated Wrist Lock.*

C–D. Attacker counters by dropping his elbow. Defender transitions to a *Gooseneck Lock.*

E–F. Attacker counters by straightening his arm. Defender transitions to an *Arm Bar.*

G–I. Attacker counters by circling ahead of the hold. Defender passes under the arm and transitions to an *Inside Twisting Arm Lock.*

14.1 Transition within the Flow of Combat (continuous sequence showing transitions to different holds as opponent counters; see explanation above)

15. Understand the Human Body

All holds, particularly joint locks, attempt to capitalize on basic anatomical limitations in the human body. If you understand these limitations, you will understand why a technique works and why it does not, and will better understand the type of force that must be applied. This requires observation and experimentation more than anything else. Understanding the structure and functions of the human body is one of the most singularly important areas of study in the martial arts—an absolute necessity if you wish to develop an efficient and compassionate approach to self-defense and combat. It is unfortunately one of the areas most ignored in training.

Anatomy as the Basis of Improvisation
Understanding anatomy is also crucially important in transitions, in which one must modify or create techniques to suit the changing flow of combat. It is likely that anatomical ignorance results in more bad technique and learning difficulties than any other single factor—in novices as well as advanced students. For example, when applying a Bent-Arm Wrist Lock, novices are taught to direct the hand toward the midline of the body for maximum efficiency. This is certainly good advice and yields positive results in most situations. However, if you understand the limitations of the wrist joint, you will realize that other options for directing force are also available. The photographs at right illustrate this point. In example A, the lock is applied by directing force toward the opponent's midline. In example B, the opponent straightens his wrist to counter the hold (this does not require a great deal of strength). Without shifting grips or stepping, redirect force by leveraging the joint sideways, toward the forearm. You can assist the technique by leveraging their fingers at the same time. This same example can be applied to numerous other situations.

A. Bent Wrist: Hand rotated toward body midline
B. Straight Wrist: Hand rotated toward forearm

14.2 Transition within the Flow of Combat *(continuous sequence showing transitions to different holds as opponent counters; see explanation on opposite page)*

16. Evaluate and Compensate

Executing a hold against a willing and cooperative partner is very different than attempting the same hold in actual combat. A skillful opponent can quickly negate even the best technique by simply resisting with force, changing leverage angles, or applying counters. Many holds that work well against equally-sized opponents quickly lose their effectiveness against larger, more powerful attackers. For example, against a powerful opponent gripping your wrist, you may not even be able to begin the necessary leading motions to enter a counterhold or escape. In these situations, you must *compensate* to equalize the differences. This can be accomplished by: selecting appropriate techniques that do not rely on physical strength; making extensive use of acupoints; channeling Ki; or executing forceful strikes to assist the technique. Finger locks are among the strongest controlling techniques, and are particularly recommended when smaller individuals are facing overpowering attackers. Chokes from an opponent's rear also work well in unequal conflicts—if you can manage to secure and maintain a strong hold.

Generally, you should always evaluate an opponent's anatomy and movements for clues revealing weaknesses. For example, someone who is overweight, possesses spindly legs, or moves awkwardly is more vulnerable to unbalancing techniques. In these situations, you might attempt to move your opponent by using pronounced leading, combined with kicks to the knee as you apply a hold.

16. Evaluate and Compensate (combining a finger lock with a kick to control an overpowering attacker)

17. Finish in a Controlling Position

Always try to finish a hold in a safe, controlled position. This usually means forcing your opponents to the ground, so they are reclining face-down (not kneeling). From this position, it will be difficult for them to punch, counter, or protect themselves from blows. Finishing a hold rarely involves both people standing, unless you are: escorting someone (usually only required in law enforcement, security and military work); or fighting multiple opponents, where time does not permit transitions to the ground. In this situation, apply the hold forcefully to break the joint, so you can quickly address the next attacker. If they fall to the ground—terrific. If they do not, they will be in far too much pain to continue the attack, or will be fighting with serious injuries.

Methods of Execution

Holds can be applied in many different situations. Some holds work well in a variety of scenarios; others are highly specialized. In self-defense oriented martial arts like Hapkido, throws are commonly practiced from three basic modes:

1. To counter a hold
2. To counter an incoming attack (strikes, pushes, attempts to grab)
3. To initiate an attack

The photos at right show an arm bar hold, applied to the situations listed above. Holds are also used to assist strikes or throws (see bottom far-right), counter joint locks or throws, or during ground fighting.

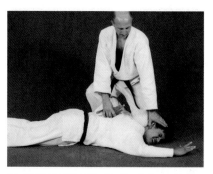

17. Finish in a Controlling Position (using a shoulder lock, nerve press, knee choke and body weight to pin)

Training Considerations

Holds are potentially devastating techniques, which can easily cause serious injury or permanent disabilities if they are forcefully applied. The following precautions and practices are suggested when training:

Pay Attention to Pain

Pain is the body's way of telling us that something isn't right. Nonetheless, you must be willing to experience a certain degree of pain for training to be realistic. Otherwise, you will never truly understand how a hold works. Tolerance of pain varies by individual. Just because a person isn't experiencing pain doesn't mean damage isn't occurring. Some individuals will not experience pain until a few minutes after a hold is applied. This failure to register pain can result from differences in individual anatomy, existing nerve damage, or the presence of drugs in the system. It also occurs when technique is poor, or the hold is used in inappropriate situations. If you are applying significant force and your partner is unaffected, *do not apply greater force* to produce pain. Have your instructor evaluate the situation. When in doubt, use less force to be safe. When training with a partner, let them tell you how much pain is tolerable. Never apply forceful chokes without qualified supervision and the presence of someone certified in *revival techniques*. Generally, most training injuries occur at the novice level, due to clumsiness and excessive force.

Practice Lightly

When learning new holds, it is important to apply enough force to know that the hold will work, with your partner resisting. However, once you understand the mechanics of a hold and can make it work well, it is not necessary to practice forcefully all the time. Practice lightly to develop speed, fluidity, and sensitivity. This also helps prevent repetitive motion from causing long-term wear and tear to your joints, leading to chronic conditions. When you are the recipient, *go with the flow* so your partner can practice a full range of motion without hurting you. This also allows you to practice motions essential to counters.

Methods of Execution

Hold countering a hold

Hold countering an incoming attack

Hold applied by initiating an attack (feinting or striking as you grab the hand)

Hold applied to assist a throw

Repetition is the Key to Perfection

Any world-class athlete in any sport knows that repetition is the key to mastery. Constant repetition ingrains biomechanical motions and physical responses that are essential to performing at the highest level. In martial arts, you must practice thousands of repetitions to perfect entries and develop fluid transitions. Proficiency in holds takes years to attain, due to the complex motions involved. Only through constant repetition can you refine, simplify, and build the auto-responses that are essential to making smooth, intuitive transitions in real situations. Eventually you should be able to execute holds blindfolded, which is also an excellent way to refine skills.

Work with Different Partners

Try to work with different practice partners rather than the same individual constantly. This will teach you to adjust for variations in size, body weight, speed, power, flexibility, and athleticism. When fighting larger persons, all holds have practical limitations, which vary by technique and individual. Only through varied practice can you come to know what these limitations are.

Summary

Holding techniques constitute one of the most complex, varied, and technically difficult technique areas to master. They require mental as well as physical ability, diligent practice, and focused concentration. The line between what works and what does not is very thin. An incorrect angle or slight error in direction can be all the difference between success and failure. For these reasons, children do not usually possess the necessary focus or concentration to master these complex techniques, as they become easily distracted or bored. Children also do not usually possess the emotional control to be safely trusted with techniques that can cause devastating destruction. In contrast, holding techniques are well suited to older individuals. While your ability to kick and punch diminishes with age, your ability to continue applying various holds will remain much longer—improving like a fine wine.

The stances you will use depend upon the techniques you are executing, the martial art you are practicing, personal preference, and a variety of other factors. It is not possible to cover all of the stances used when executing martial holds, as there are simply too many variables. Nonetheless, there are a few fundamental stances that are found in many practical or self-defense oriented martial arts. They are shown opposite. Generally speaking, it is better to think of stances as the links in a series of continuous movements, rather than as precisely defined foot placements. A rigid approach only limits your technique and your ability to adapt and improvise based on the constantly changing dynamics of combat. Most stances fall into two basic categories: relaxed stances and fighting stances.

Relaxed Stances
Relaxed stances resemble everyday standing or sitting postures. Since one never knows when they might be attacked, reacting and applying self-defense techniques from relaxed stances is an important skill for students to learn. Self-defense oriented martial arts, such as Hapkido, also make significant use of relaxed stances to camouflage tactics and lure an opponent into a false sense of security. Attacking and defending from relaxed stances is also useful when one wishes to maintain a low profile or minimize disturbance to people nearby.

Fighting Stances
In fighting stances, the position of the hands, feet, and body is optimized to facilitate execution of techniques. There are many types of fighting stances. The three shown at right are found in many practical martial arts. These stances can be used in a wide variety of circumstances to launch a broad range of techniques, such as strikes, kicks, holds, chokes, and throws. The Front Stance tends to be more offensive, whereas the Back Stance usually favors defense. The Grappling Stance is often used when two combatants have already secured grips on one another. At that point, mobility is less important than stability.

1. Relaxed Standing Stance

Weight Distribution: Equal between both feet. This basic ready stance is often used to disguise tactics and intent. Place your feet shoulder-width apart with the knees slightly bent. Hands are open and hanging loosely at side. The entire body should be relaxed, ready to quickly respond. Do not adopt any hand or foot positions that could be construed as a preparation to attack. Face is expressionless. This stance is also called a *Natural Stance*.

2. Relaxed Walking Stance

Weight Distribution: Constantly changing. This posture is actually a form of offensive movement as well as a stance. It is used to disguise tactics and intent while being constantly mobile. Adopt a normal walk with relaxed arms and legs swinging freely and naturally. The flowing continuous movement of the hands, arms, and feet make this an excellent posture for launching disguised strikes, blocks, holds, or throws.

Foot diagrams refer to top photograph and indicate preferred foot positions. However, these positions are always modified based on end-use requirements. Black dot indicates center of gravity based on weight distribution given in the text. When a range is given, a black and a white dot indicate the range.

3. Front Stance

Weight Distribution: 50–60% front foot.
This basic fighting stance is highly mobile, and good for fast footwork and entering. It is excellent for launching strikes, holds, or throws, but lacks stability if you are grappling at close range. Position the feet about 1 to 1.5 times your shoulder-width apart. The back foot may be flat or raised on the ball. This stance is commonly seen in a variety of styles, from boxing to Olympic Taekwondo.

4. Back Stance

Weight Distribution: 50–75% back foot.
This basic defensive stance possesses a good balance between stability and mobility. More weight on the back foot favors defense and use of the front leg for countering and blocking. Position the feet about 1.5 times your shoulder-width, with both legs bent. The front foot points straight forward, the rear foot points sideways (slightly less than 90°), the heels align. Shoulders and hips align with feet.

5. Grappling Stance

Weight Distribution: Equal between both feet.
This basic defensive stance is used when grappling, holding, or throwing. It can be very stable, but possesses low mobility. Position the feet about 1.5 times your shoulder-width, with the toes turned outward and legs equally bent. Align the shoulders and hips with the feet. Center of gravity and hip placement are fairly low, to prevent being unbalanced or thrown by a grappling opponent.

1. Forward Step

6. Back Shuffle

11. Side Slide (front left)

16. Side Slide–Step (right)

2. Forward Slide

7. Side Step–Front Pivot (left)

12. Side Slide (front right)

17. Turn Step (face forward)

3. Forward Shuffle

8. Side Step–Front Pivot (right)

13. Side Slide (back left)

18. Turn Step (face behind)

4. Back Step

9. Side Step–Back Pivot (left)

14. Side Slide (back right)

19. Pivot (face side)

5. Back Slide

10. Side Step–Back Pivot (right)

15. Side Slide–Step (left)

20. Pivot (face behind)

Most standing footwork derives from about 40 basic steps, which are combined or altered to create innumerable possibilities. During grappling, short steps with wider stances are usually preferred for stability and to prevent an opponent from sweeping your feet or throwing you. Steps 31–40 are variations modified for close-range grappling.

Outlined feet indicate start position; *solid* feet indicate ending. Numbers indicate which foot moves first.

P Pivot
B Back Foot
F Front Foot
1, 2 Sequence

21. Step-Pivot (front step)

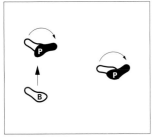

22. Step-Pivot (back step)

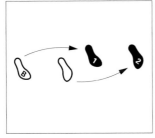

23. Front Draw

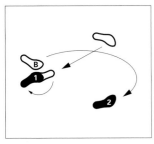

24. Front Draw Turning

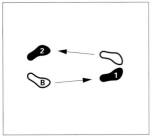

25. Rear Draw

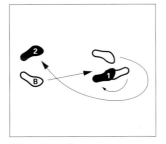

26. Rear Draw Turning

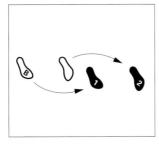

27. Cross Step Behind

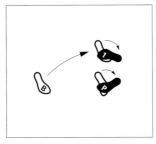

28. Cross Step Front

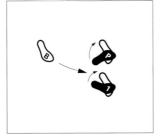

29. Cross Step Behind–Pivot

30. Cross Step Front–Pivot

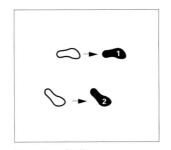

31. Forward Shuffle

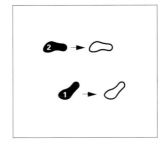

32. Back Shuffle

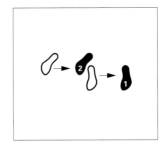

33. Side Shuffle

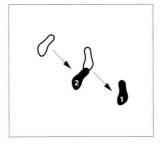

34. Diagonal Shuffle

35. Forward Turn (left pivot)

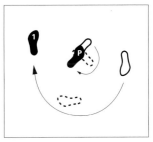

36. Forward Turn (right pivot)

37. Back Turn (left pivot)

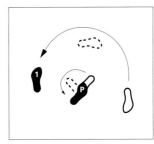

38. Back Turn (right pivot)

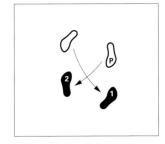

39. Two Step Turn (left)

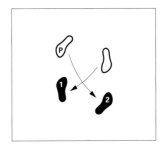

40. Two Step Turn (right)

COMBINATION STEPS

The basic steps shown on the previous pages are often linked into sequences. Typical combination steps used when grappling are:

Blending Footwork

Blending footwork combines several of the basic steps covered previously, and is mostly used to position your body outside an attacker's force. When stepping you may avoid, redirect, or join with the attack, depending on your tactics. Blending footwork is used in conjunction with strikes, blocks, holds, or throws (particularly unbalancing throws). The footwork can be executed from any stance or combination of stances.

Two common blending footwork sequences are shown below. They are a combination of several basic steps described previously. Example 1 combines a forward step (#1) and a turn step (#17). Example 2 combines a side step (#11) and a turn step (#17). Many other variations are possible. These sequences are generally characterized by turning and circular movement. When executing blending footwork, move quickly and lightly on the balls of the feet, keep the hips high and knees flexed, and use the shoulders and hips to assist body rotation. Make one continuous movement without any pauses. To develop flexibility, speed, and fluidity, practice using a variety of stances and techniques.

Pivoting Footwork

Pivoting footwork is primarily used to alternately turn and face multiple opponents, while maintaining a stationary position. In pivoting footwork, step with one foot while constantly pivoting on the other foot. There are two basic variations: pivoting on the back foot while stepping with the front foot, or pivoting on the front foot while stepping with the back foot (you can also mix both variations together). This footwork can be executed from any stance or combination of stances. Pivoting footwork consists of basic steps #35 and #38. The height of your center of gravity (hips) varies depending upon tactics and stance selection.

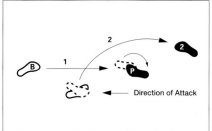
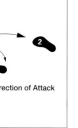

1. Blending footwork beginning with forward step

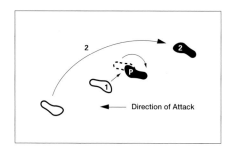

2. Blending footwork beginning with side step

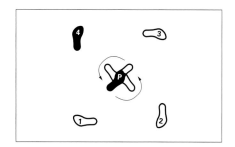

3. Pivoting to face multiple opponents

Entering + Pivoting Footwork

This type of footwork is used to position your body and execute a pivot (usually 90–180°). It usually consists of two steps, although there are many variations. In some holds, the body pivot is also used to power the hold. Two common examples of entering and pivoting footwork, used in many holds, are shown below. Further explanation follows:

Explanation for Sequence 4

From a Relaxed Stance (A), step 45° forward to your right with your right foot, planting it outside the opponent's left foot (B). Cross step behind your right foot with your left foot (C), and pivot 180° as you apply the hold (D).

Explanation for Sequence 5

From a Relaxed Stance, step 45° forward to your left with your right foot, planting it with your toes turned outward and the heel turned inward (B). Step to your right with your left foot, pivoting 180° as you step under the arm (C). Execute the hold (D–E). The turned right foot assists the pivoting motion that occurs as you step with your left foot. Many martial artists perform this step without turning their toes outward (B), which also works well. However, this method is arguably slower and requires upweighting to reduce stress on the knee and increase pivoting speed. To use the upweighting method, raise your hips slightly as you pivot, by extending your legs. This momentarily reduces the weight on your feet, which in turn reduces friction between your pivoting sole and the ground. This is similar to the manner in which a skier initiates turns.

Footwork Practice

Fast, fluid footwork is developed by practicing basic steps and then gradually combining them into sequences designed to respond to specific conditions. Thousands of repetitions are normally required to program the body's auto responses. Good footwork can be developed by working alone, but is best developed through free-sparring or competition, since there you must learn to anticipate and react instinctively to constantly changing factors.

4. *Typical example of entering and pivoting footwork used to execute a Two-Hand Arm Bar*

5. *Typical example of entering and pivoting footwork used to execute an Outside Twisting Arm Lock*

Breakfalls

Many holds can be used to force a takedown or violently hurl an opponent to the ground, much the same as throwing arts. If you do not know how to fall, many holds and throws will produce serious injuries. A *breakfall* is a specific method of falling, designed to protect your body from damage as you hit the ground. This involves specific formations of your body which minimize impact by dispersing force over a large surface area. Eight basic types of breakfalls, common to many martial arts, are shown on subsequent pages. The photo(s) above each sequence shows each breakfall being used during a typical technique. Although breakfalls are usually associated with throwing arts, they are also necessary when defending against certain holds. When learning holding and throwing arts, breakfalls are among the first skills that should be taught. All breakfalls should be learned from a qualified instructor, since improperly executed breakfalls can easily result in injuries.

During self-defense or combat, the breakfall you will use is based on how you are held or thrown. In all breakfalls, you will attempt to control your body position while airborne. As your body lands in the proper position, you will usually *slap* and emit an *energy-shout* at the same time. In some martial arts an energy-shout is not used; practitioners will instead either exhale or hold their breath.

The Slap

In most breakfalls you will slap with your hand and forearm, or entire arm, to distribute the force of impact. This also helps to position your body and assists in timing. The force of your slap must be adjusted based on the hardness of the surface you are falling onto. While it is common to see students endlessly practicing forceful slaps on the mat, these same slaps will cause you to injure or break your hand when falling on hard surfaces like concrete. In some soft-style martial arts, the slap is barely articulated or nonexistent, since the focus is on blending with the ground.

The Energy-Shout

An energy-shout is an abrupt shout designed to focus your energy and power, and was covered previously in this chapter, under *Energetic Concepts.* During breakfalls, an energy-shout helps protect the body from injury, keeps the wind from being knocked out of your lungs, and causes your body to naturally relax on impact. Some martial arts do not use a shout, but instead focus on relaxing and blending with the ground. In some Chinese arts, practitioners are taught to tense their body and hold their breath during a breakfall, the idea being that this prevents organ damage from the force of impact.

Self-Initiated Breakfalls

In some martial arts, such as Hapkido, you will often initiate your own fall, to counter joint locks or throws. This saves your joints from serious injury, and propels you ahead of an attacker's force. Self-initiated breakfalls are the basis of many counters and escapes.

An example is shown at the bottom of the next page. If these opponents did not execute breakfalls, they would suffer serious injuries.

Improvised Breakfalls

In the beginning, good form is important to prevent injury. As you obtain experience, you will notice that there are many ways to fall, some quite unorthodox. In the end, how you fall is irrelevant, since the ultimate objective is to survive and consistently remain injury free. If you have existing injuries and wish to continue training, modified breakfalls are often required to protect those parts of your body that are already damaged. For example, if your finger(s) are broken or your arm is injured, eliminate the slap. Most practitioners who omit the slap, usually notice very little difference in force of impact, since body positioning is far more critical than slapping. Modified breakfalls may also be required if one of your limbs is being held or restrained, as shown in the photos at right.

In this double-hold, two opponent's are executing Back Falls to keep their shoulders from being dislocated.

Improvised breakfalls: In this photo, twin finger-locks force two attackers to fall forward. The attackers must execute modified Front Falls with one-hand only (other hands are held).

Self-initiated breakfalls are often required to save your joints from serious injury. This photo shows two attackers executing Flip Side Falls.

1. Front Fall

As you fall forward, position your hands in front of your face, with your bent-arms at a 45° angle, hands aligned with forearms. While airborne, spread your feet shoulder-width apart or wider. As you approach the ground, slap downward with both hands and forearms, as you shout or exhale. Your hands should make contact slightly before your forearms. The underside of your toes should make contact at the same time.

Important Points

As you fall, turn your head sideways to avoid accidentally breaking your nose. Do not allow your knees or torso to hit the ground. Try to absorb some of the shock by flexing your elbows and shoulders as you land. *Do not* land directly on the elbows (fracture), or reach out with your palms (broken wrist). When first learning to fall, practice from a kneeling position, progressing to squatting, then standing, and eventually airborne.

2. Soft Front Fall

As you fall forward, reach out for the ground with both hands and withdraw them as your hands make contact. Slow your descent by using your arm and shoulder muscles to lower your chest to the ground. This is similar to doing a *push-up*. Simultaneously, arch your back to slow the descent of your legs, landing on the underside of your toes, with your feet shoulder-width apart or wider. Turn your head to protect your nose.

Important Points

This form of breakfall has become more popular in recent years, since it transmits less shock to the arms and shoulders during impact. This makes it more suitable for older individuals, or people who have initial fears about learning to fall. However, there are many situations when it is not possible to control your landing in this manner. Learning the previous *Front Fall* is still considered very important.

3. Back Fall

As you fall backward, cross your arms and tuck your chin against your chest, to keep your head from hitting the ground. As you land on the back of your shoulders, slap the ground with both hands and arms at a 45° angle from your body, and shout or exhale. Quickly retract your hands to prepare for your next technique. When falling from a standing posture (see photos), keep your hips close to your heels.

Important Points

Do not slap higher than 45°. It is ineffective, and will often stress the shoulders, or cause the wind to be knocked out of you. Keep your back curved as you fall. When first learning, progress from lying to sitting, to squatting, to standing, then airborne. Try to avoid landing on the middle or lower back, since this stresses the spine. High falls can be difficult, since minor errors often result in neck or back injuries.

4. Bridge Fall

This breakfall is used when you are flipped straight over onto your back. You will land on the back of your shoulders and balls of your feet, thus avoiding serious injury to your spine. As you land, tuck your chin, elevate the buttocks, slap the ground with both hands and arms at a 45° angle from your body, and shout or exhale. Quickly retract your hands to prepare for your next technique.

Important Points

Do not land on your heels, since this transmits substantial shock to your ankles and knees, and the nerves at the bottom of your heel. When first learning this fall, practice by executing a forward roll very low to the ground. Then progress to flipping straight over with your arms straight and the body extended (see photos). Eventually you can practice airborne falls without using your hands for support.

5. Sit-Out Side Fall

This breakfall is used when you are falling to your side or rear-corner. As one leg is swept or reaped, you will lower yourself using your supporting leg. Sit back toward your rear-corner, rolling onto your side, as you slap the ground with one arm at a 45° angle from your body, and shout or exhale. Allow the rolling motion to carry your legs upward. The slap is often not needed, but helps time your actions.

Important Points

This is a very low-impact fall, since you are controlling your own descent throughout. It sometimes helps to think of it as a *back roll* executed on the side of your body. Keep your buttock close to your heel as you sit back. This breakfall is often confused with the next technique, however, they are quite different. In this breakfall, one leg supports your fall. In the *Sweep Side Fall*, both feet leave the ground.

6. Sweep Side Fall

This breakfall is used when one or both legs are swept out from under you. You will land on the side of your body, as you slap the ground with one arm (at a 45° angle from the body) and shout or exhale. The entire right side of your body and your left foot contact the ground at the same time. The left leg is bent and vertical, landing on the ball of the foot. The right leg is slightly bent, with the sole turned up to protect the ankle.

Important Points

Make sure you tuck your chin, turn your right foot upward to protect your protruding ankle from hitting the ground, and land on the back of your right shoulder—not the side, or serious injury will result. When compared to the previous *Sit-Out Side Fall*, this fall involves greater impact, with both legs contacting the ground. The force of the throw will not allow you to *sit-out* as described in the previous breakfall.

7. Flip Side Fall

This breakfall is used when your are flipped straight over onto your side. As you land, slap the ground with one arm at a 45° angle from your body, and shout or exhale. The entire right side of your body and your left foot contact the ground at the same time. Your left leg is bent and vertical, landing on the ball of the foot. Your right leg is either slightly bent with the sole turned up, or fully bent with the heel near the buttock.

Important Points

This breakfall is used during most hip and shoulder throws, or when initiating your own fall to counter a joint lock. There are two common leg formations used when landing. The only difference is the position of your left leg. The *Extended-Leg Landing* is more common, and is also used in the Sweep Side Fall. In the *Bent-Leg Landing,* you will fully retract your left leg, being careful not to strike your left ankle with your right heel.

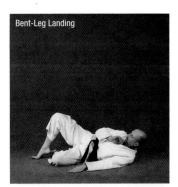
Bent-Leg Landing

Extended-Leg Landing

---

8. Twisting Side Fall

This breakfall is used when one arm is held behind your back, and you are forced to fall on that same side. Twist your upper body as you fall, bending your legs to control your descent. Land on the side of your right leg, as you slap with your left hand and forearm, and shout or exhale. Twisting your upper body is crucial to prevent your right shoulder from slamming into the ground. Turn your head to protect your nose.

Important Points

This breakfall is rarely needed, which may be the reason it is not taught in most schools. However, during certain types of falls resulting from *Hammer Locks* or *Twisting Arm Locks,* it may provide your only sensible means of protection. In these situations, your opponent may be trying to get you to fall directly onto your shoulder, or backward onto your own arm—resulting in serious injuries (usually to the shoulder).

1. Forward Shoulder Roll

A forward shoulder roll can be used for a variety of offensive and defensive purposes. It is used for protection when being thrown, for movement on the ground, to execute dropping kicks, and for making transitions from reclining to standing postures, or standing to reclining postures. If you are thrown forcefully forward or from a height, you must roll to prevent injury. This is a function of physics: the spinning motion significantly reduces friction and initial impact by redirecting your force upon contact with the ground. When shoulder rolling, the human body resembles a spinning ball glancing across a surface.

Executing a Shoulder Roll

A. Step forward with one foot leading, feet shoulder-width apart. Your leading arm will be used to enter the roll and is always on the same side as the leading foot. The outside of your arm and the knife-edge of your hand are turned outward toward the ground, with the elbow and wrist slightly bent, forming a curved arc with the arm.

B–C. Bend forward, thrust your lead hand forward, down and back between your legs in a vertical circular motion (as if reaching around a barrel). Your entire body follows this motion. Coordinating arm movement with the vertical rotation of the hips and shoulders is essential for generating motion. The trailing hand may be used for support if desired. The fingers are placed on the ground pointing forward (palm elevated), with your hand forming a triangle with both feet. As shoulder rolls increase in height and distance, use of both hands for catching, absorbing, and guiding the roll becomes essential.

D–E. Roll along the outside of your arm and shoulder, on a diagonal across your upper back to the opposite hip and leg (e.g., leading with the left arm means exiting on the right hip and leg). Tuck your chin against the chest. The head and lower spine never touch the ground. Both arms appear to form a circle.

F–G. Upon exiting the roll, keep both legs bent in one of the leg formations described in the next paragraph. Use your forward momentum to resume a kneeling or standing position, or to continue rolling. You may also exit a roll into a Seated Guard or side fall. This may become necessary if you wish to remain on the ground, or have been thrown and your opponent continues to hold your arm.

Leg Formations When Exiting

You may exit a forward roll using either a bent-leg or an extended-leg formation. In the *bent-leg* formation the leading leg is vertical, with the knee bent at least 90°. The trailing leg is fully bent and folded under, horizontal

1. Forward Shoulder Roll

Forward shoulder roll using bent-leg exit

Forward shoulder roll using extended-leg exit (note use of hand)

and flush against ground. This leg arrangement is also used in certain types of breakfalls (see Flip Side Fall); it is often called a *figure 4*, since it resembles the shape of that number. The bent-leg formation is generally preferred for rolling, as it naturally leads to kneeling or standing postures, keeps the hands free to attack or defend, positions the legs for a Seated Guard or immediate kick, facilitates transitions into additional rolls, and reduces side stress on the trailing knee. On hard surfaces, the protruding bent-leg ankle bone is prone to damage from contact with the ground. Try to minimize ankle contact by first absorbing impact with the lower leg, or use the extended-leg version.

In the *extended-leg* formation the trailing leg is partially bent and placed alongside the bent vertical lead leg. This variation is usually used when exiting into a side fall, or if you wish to remain on the ground. Rising to a standing posture is more difficult without use of the hands or greater rotational force. When rolling on hard surfaces, the ankle is better protected than in the bent-leg formation.

2. Back Shoulder Roll

Back shoulder rolls are used for the same purposes as forward shoulder rolls. They are also used during sacrifice throws or as part of a sit-out entry into a seated guard. A back roll is basically a forward shoulder roll in reverse.

Executing a Back Roll

A–B. Sit back from a standing posture, lowering yourself to the ground by using a two-foot, bent-leg, or extended-leg entry.

C–D. Form your body into a tight ball, keeping the back rounded and head tucked. Sit back, rolling across either shoulder. As you exit the roll, place the opposite hand (left shoulder, right hand) on the ground for support.

E. Exit the roll, landing directly on the balls of the feet and palms of the hand. Resume a kneeling or standing position.

Back Roll Entry Options

You may enter a back roll using either a two-foot entry, extended-leg entry, or a bent-leg entry (see photos below). The version selected depends upon individual preference or the techniques to which the move is linked. For example, a *two-foot entry* is often selected when both feet will be used simultaneously from a ground position (e.g., twin kicks). An *extended-leg entry* might be used to execute a kick while falling, or when one knee is damaged and can't be bent. A *bent-leg entry* is often used while stepping backward. All three entries can be linked to specific sacrifice throws and ground fighting skills. It is wise to practice all three methods so that you have suitable options for any situation that may arise.

2. Back shoulder roll using two-foot entry

Back shoulder roll using extended-leg entry

Back shoulder roll using bent-leg entry

3. Forward Roll

A *forward roll* and a *forward shoulder roll* are entirely different techniques, although the terms are often used interchangeably. In a forward roll, the body is facing straight ahead (no lead leg) and the roll is executed symmetrically by rolling from both shoulders down the length of the back. Both hands, rather than one arm, initially guide the roll. A forward roll can be used for the same purposes as a forward shoulder roll, although it is more difficult to execute safely from heights or when being thrown. In most martial arts, it is not used as frequently as the shoulder roll, although in some situations it is quite useful.

A forward roll is normally used when it is not possible to position or guide the upper body properly for a shoulder roll. It is also commonly used when first teaching students the fundamentals of rolling, since it is more psychologically comfortable for people who have no prior experience tumbling.

Executing a Forward Roll
A–B. Place both hands flat on the ground, with the arms slightly bent. Tuck the head by placing the chin against the chest. Form the body into a tight ball by rounding the spine.

C–D. Bend forward, projecting the hips directly overhead. Use both hands to lower and guide your body into the roll, making contact on the upper back and shoulders,

down the spine and buttocks, and exiting onto the soles of both feet. The head must never touch the ground, or you risk damaging the cervical spine or its nerve roots.

E. Upon exiting, keep both legs bent and the body tightly tucked, with the hands and arms extended forward. Use your momentum to stand or to continue rolling. Avoid using your hands to assist exiting from the roll, since they may be required for attacking, defending, or generating the next movement. Reaching back to push yourself forward also stops the forward motion of the shoulders and upper body, which is essential for completing the roll and returning to your feet.

4. Side Roll

A side roll is used to move laterally from kneeling and reclining postures. It is often used to avoid an attack or move away from standing opponents, after you have been thrown. If you are ground fighting against multiple opponents, side rolls will allow you to face 180° opposite (see steps A–C).

Executing a Side Roll
Pull the leading arm in tight to the body, roll across the back, and keep your knees tucked. In the sequences shown, the roll is executed with both legs bent. During the roll you will make contact with both knees and the balls of the feet. If you were rolling from a reclining position, the legs can be extended. There are many variations on the basic roll shown.

5–7 Recovering a Standing Position

Recovery techniques are usually used to regain a standing posture after falling or being thrown. Speed, timing, and economy of movement are crucial, since you may be under constant attack. Common methods are:

5. Roll-Up Recovery

This is basically the end of a forward roll. Generate momentum by rocking backward, then forward. With legs fully bent, pull both feet to your buttocks, keeping them slightly wider than shoulder-width apart. Whip the upper body and arms forward, drawing the chest to the knees, as you roll up onto both feet. If you find yourself falling backward, you have probably placed your feet too close together, failed to generate sufficient momentum, or are not tightly tucked.

6. Back Shoulder Roll Recovery

This movement is used to move backward while changing from a reclining or kneeling position to standing. It is used to create distance, avoid an attack, or initiate a retreat.

7. Two-Hand Recovery

This technique is used to regain a standing position after taking a side fall. To execute, support yourself with one or both hands as you bring the extended leg back to the rear. Do not move the other leg, as it is already properly positioned. Transfer your weight to both feet, bringing the hands up to a guard position for protection, as you stand up.

3. Forward Roll

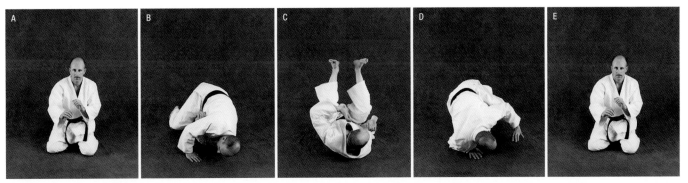

4. Side Roll (from Two Knee Stance)

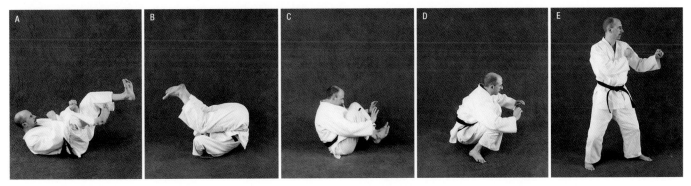

5. Roll-Up Recovery

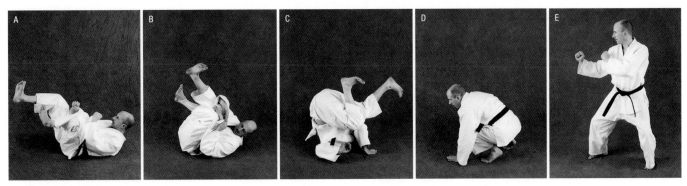

6. Back Shoulder Roll Recovery

7. Two-Hand Recovery (from extended-leg side fall)

PRESSURE POINT TARGETS

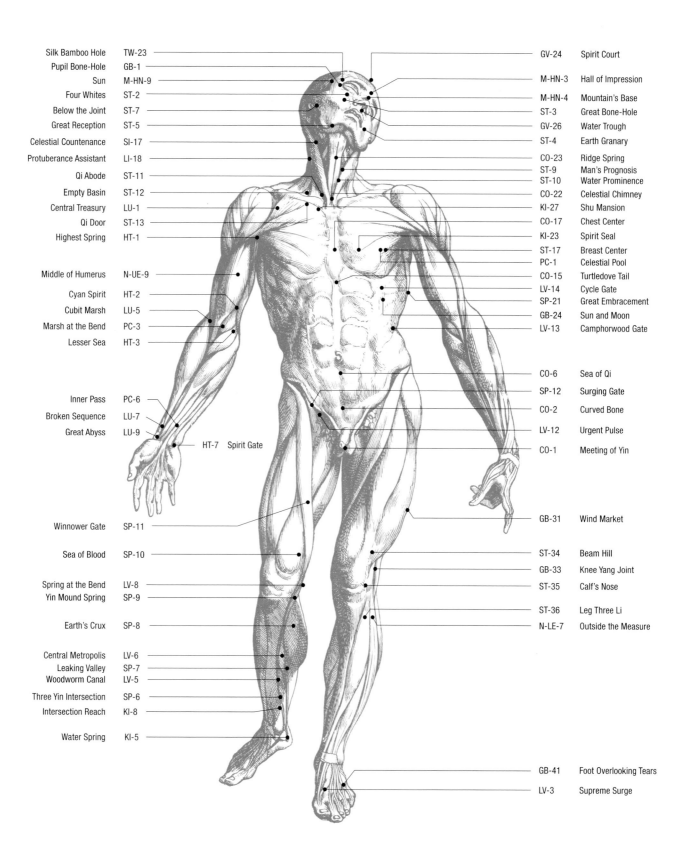

Silk Bamboo Hole	TW-23		GV-24	Spirit Court
Pupil Bone-Hole	GB-1		M-HN-3	Hall of Impression
Sun	M-HN-9		M-HN-4	Mountain's Base
Four Whites	ST-2		ST-3	Great Bone-Hole
Below the Joint	ST-7		GV-26	Water Trough
Great Reception	ST-5		ST-4	Earth Granary
Celestial Countenance	SI-17		CO-23	Ridge Spring
Protuberance Assistant	LI-18		ST-9	Man's Prognosis
Qi Abode	ST-11		ST-10	Water Prominence
Empty Basin	ST-12		CO-22	Celestial Chimney
Central Treasury	LU-1		KI-27	Shu Mansion
Qi Door	ST-13		CO-17	Chest Center
Highest Spring	HT-1		KI-23	Spirit Seal
			ST-17	Breast Center
			PC-1	Celestial Pool
Middle of Humerus	N-UE-9		CO-15	Turtledove Tail
Cyan Spirit	HT-2		LV-14	Cycle Gate
Cubit Marsh	LU-5		SP-21	Great Embracement
Marsh at the Bend	PC-3		GB-24	Sun and Moon
Lesser Sea	HT-3		LV-13	Camphorwood Gate
			CO-6	Sea of Qi
Inner Pass	PC-6		SP-12	Surging Gate
Broken Sequence	LU-7		CO-2	Curved Bone
Great Abyss	LU-9		LV-12	Urgent Pulse
	HT-7	Spirit Gate	CO-1	Meeting of Yin
Winnower Gate	SP-11		GB-31	Wind Market
Sea of Blood	SP-10		ST-34	Beam Hill
			GB-33	Knee Yang Joint
Spring at the Bend	LV-8		ST-35	Calf's Nose
Yin Mound Spring	SP-9			
			ST-36	Leg Three Li
Earth's Crux	SP-8		N-LE-7	Outside the Measure
Central Metropolis	LV-6			
Leaking Valley	SP-7			
Woodworm Canal	LV-5			
Three Yin Intersection	SP-6			
Intersection Reach	KI-8			
Water Spring	KI-5			
			GB-41	Foot Overlooking Tears
			LV-3	Supreme Surge

The illustrations on these pages show 106 common pressure point targets used in the martial arts. Each point is labeled using both its alphanumeric symbol, and the English translation of the point's Chinese name. Korean and Japanese translations are usually similar, if not identical. *Essential Anatomy for Healing and Martial Arts*, by the same author, contains additional pressure point targets and charts, a detailed discussion of pressure point fighting principles, a comprehensive presentation of human anatomy in both Eastern and Western medical systems, and an index listing the precise anatomical location of more than 380 pressure points, cross-referenced to nerves, blood vessels, and other anatomical landmarks.

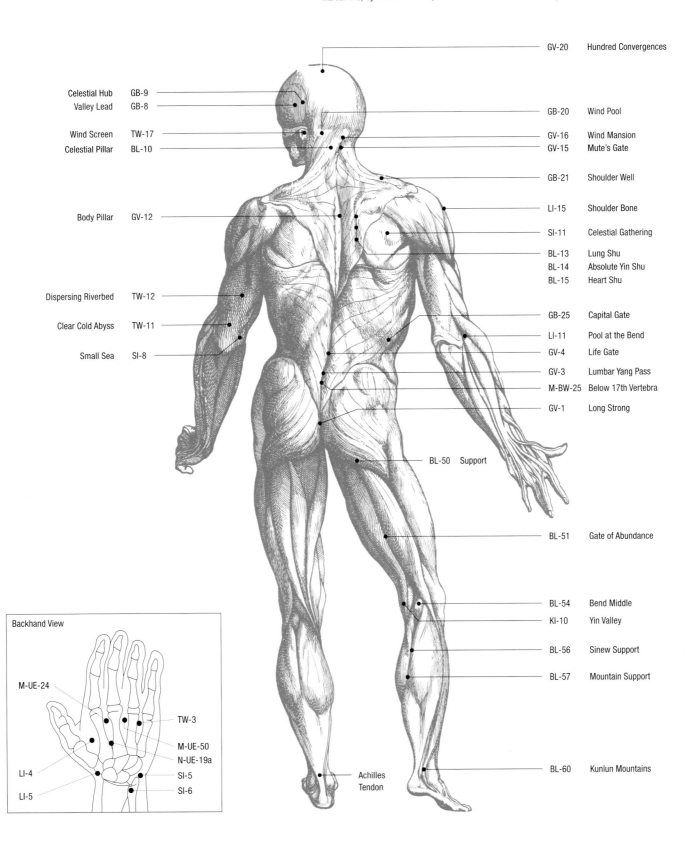

	GV-20	Hundred Convergences
Celestial Hub	GB-9	
Valley Lead	GB-8	
	GB-20	Wind Pool
Wind Screen	TW-17	GV-16 Wind Mansion
Celestial Pillar	BL-10	GV-15 Mute's Gate
	GB-21	Shoulder Well
	LI-15	Shoulder Bone
Body Pillar	GV-12	SI-11 Celestial Gathering
	BL-13	Lung Shu
	BL-14	Absolute Yin Shu
	BL-15	Heart Shu
Dispersing Riverbed	TW-12	GB-25 Capital Gate
Clear Cold Abyss	TW-11	LI-11 Pool at the Bend
Small Sea	SI-8	GV-4 Life Gate
	GV-3	Lumbar Yang Pass
	M-BW-25	Below 17th Vertebra
	GV-1	Long Strong
	BL-50	Support
	BL-51	Gate of Abundance
	BL-54	Bend Middle
	KI-10	Yin Valley
	BL-56	Sinew Support
	BL-57	Mountain Support
	BL-60	Kunlun Mountains

Achilles Tendon

Backhand View

M-UE-24
TW-3
M-UE-50
N-UE-19a
LI-4
SI-5
LI-5
SI-6

BL-10	Back of neck, 1.3 units lateral to GV-15, within hairline, on lateral side of trapezius muscle.
BL-13	Upper back, 1.5 units lateral to lower edge of spinous process of 3rd thoracic vertebra.
BL-14	Upper back, 1.5 units lateral to lower edge of spinous process of 4th thoracic vertebra.
BL-15	Upper back, 1.5 units lateral to lower edge of spinous process of 5th thoracic vertebra.
BL-50	Buttock, at midpoint of crease below buttock (transverse gluteal crease).
BL-51	Back of thigh, 6 units below BL-50 on line joining BL-50 to BL-54.
BL-54	Back of knee, midpoint of transverse crease, between biceps + semitendinosus m. tendons.
BL-56	Lower leg, 3 units above BL-57, in center of belly of gastrocnemius m. (calf).
BL-57	Lower leg, directly below belly of gastrocnemius muscle, on line joining BL-54 to Achilles tendon.
BL-60	Outer ankle, recess halfway between protruding bone at ankle and Achilles tendon, level with tip.
CO-1	In center of perineum, between anus and genitals.
CO-2	Front midline, directly above pubic bone (pubic symphysis), 5 units below navel, (pulse is felt).
CO-6	Front midline of abdomen, 1.5 units below navel.
CO-15	Front midline, 7 units above navel, usually below xiphoid process (depends on length of cartilage).
CO-17	Front midline of chest, level with 4th intercostal space, level and between nipples, on sternum.
CO-22	Front midline, at center of sternal notch (top edge of sternum, at base of throat).
CO-23	Front midline of throat, above Adam's apple, in recess at upper edge of hyoid bone.
GB-1	About 0.5 unit lateral to outer corner of eye, in recess on lateral side of orbit (bony eye socket).
GB-8	Side of head, above apex of ear, in recess 1.5 units within hairline (point is felt when biting).
GB-9	Side of head, above and behind ear, 2 units within hairline, about 0.5 unit behind GB-8.
GB-20	Back of neck, below occipital bone, in recess between sternoceidomastoid m. and trapezius m.
GB-21	Shoulder, halfway between C7 vertebra and protruding bone at top of shoulder (acromion).
GB-24	Below nipple, between cartilage of 7th+8th ribs, one rib space below and slightly lateral to LV-14.

GB-25	Side of trunk, at lower edge of floating end of 12th rib (lowest rib).
GB-31	Outer thigh, 7 units above kneecap, at end of middle finger when arm hangs at side.
GB-33	Outer thigh, in recess above bony knob of femur, between bone and biceps femoris tendon.*
GB-41	Top of foot, in recess distal and between junction of 4th and 5th metatarsal bones.
GV-1	Halfway between tip of tailbone (coccyx) and anus.
GV-3	Midline of back, below spinous process of 4th lumbar vertebra.
GV-4	Midline of back, below spinous process of 2nd lumbar vertebra.
GV-12	Midline of back, below spinous process of 3rd thoracic vertebra.
GV-15	Back midline of neck, in recess 0.5 unit below GV-16, 0.5 unit within hairline.
GV-16	Midline of neck, in recess below ext. occipital protuberance, at trapezius muscle attachments.
GV-20	Midline of head, 7 units above rear hairline, on midpoint of line joining earlobes and ear apexes.
GV-24	Midline, on top of head, 0.5 unit within front hairline.
GV-26	Front midline, in center of groove below nose (philtrum), slightly above midpoint.
HT-1	With arm raised, in center of axilla (armpit), on medial side of axillary artery.
HT-2	3 units above medial end of elbow crease and HT-3, in groove medial to biceps muscle.
HT-3	With elbow bent, at medial end of elbow crease, in recess anterior to protruding bone at elbow.
HT-7	On transverse wrist crease, in recess between ulna and pisiform bones, radial side of tendon.
KI-5	Inner heel, in recess above and in front of bulge in heel bone, 1 unit below level of ankle.
KI-8	Inner lower leg, 2 units above level of protruding bone at ankle, posterior to medial edge of tibia.
KI-10	Medial side of back of knee, between semitendinosus + semimembranosus tendons, level BL-54.
KI-23	Chest, in 4th intercostal space (between ribs), 2 units lateral to body midline, level with nipple.
KI-27	Chest, in recess at lower edge of medial head of clavicle, 2 units lateral to body midline.
LI-4	Center of muscle between 1st + 2nd metacarpals on back of hand (web of thumb), slightly to 2nd.

LI-5	Radial side of wrist, in recess between extensor muscle tendons at base of thumb.
LI-11	In recess at lateral end of elbow crease, midway between LU-5 and protruding humerus bone.
LI-15	With arm raised, in a recess at edge of shoulder joint, slightly forward to middle of deltoid muscle.
LI-18	Side of neck, level with Adam's apple tip, directly below ear, on rear part of sternoceidomastoid m.
LU-1	Chest, 1 unit below lateral end of clavicle, in first intercostal space, 6 units lateral midline (pulse).
LU-5	Crease of elbow, at radial side of biceps tendon, at origin of brachioradialis muscle.
LU-7	Thumb-side of forearm, in crevice at lateral edge of radius bone, 1.5 units above wrist crease.
LU-9	Wrist at transverse crease, in recess on radial side of radial artery, where pulse is felt.
LV-3	Top of foot, in recess distal and between junction of 1st and 2nd metatarsal bones (above web).
LV-5	5 units above tip of protruding bone at inner ankle, between posterior edge of tibia and calf m.
LV-6	Inner ankle, 7 units above tip of protruding bone at inner ankle, on posterior edge of tibia.
LV-8	Inner knee joint. When bent, point is at medial end of crease, above tendons attaching at joint.
LV-12	Inguinal groove, 2.5 units lateral to midline, lateral to pubic symphysis, 5 units below navel.
LV-13	Trunk, below free end of 11th floating rib, 2 units above level of navel, 6 units lateral to midline.
LV-14	Chest, near medial end of 6th intercostal space (between ribs), 2 ribs below nipple.
M-BW-25	Back midline, 1 vertebra below GV-3, at lumbosacral joint (5th lumbar and 1st sacral vertebras).
M-HN-3	Front midline, in recess halfway between medial ends of eyebrows (glabella), also called GV-24.5.
M-HN-4	Front midline, lowest point on bridge of nose, halfway between inner canthi of left + right eyes.
M-HN-9	Temple, in recess 1 unit posterior to the midpoint between outer canthus of eye and tip of eyebrow.
M-UE-24	Back of hand, between 2nd and 3rd metacarpal bones, 0.5 unit proximal to base joints of fingers.
M-UE-50	Back of hand, between 3rd and 4th metacarpal bones, 0.5 unit proximal to base joints of fingers.
N-LE-7	Outer lower leg below knee, 1 unit lateral to ST-36.
N-UE-9	Front upper arm, in center of biceps brachii muscle, 4.5 units below axillary (armpit) fold.

N-UE-19a	Back of hand, at forked recess where 2nd and 3rd metacarpal bones merge.	SP-9	In recess below protruding tibia at inner knee, between rear edge of tibia and gastrocnemius m.	ST-11	Front base of neck, in recess between two heads of sternocleidomastoid m., at end of clavicle.
PC-1	Chest, 1 unit lateral to nipple, in 4th intercostal space.	SP-10	Thigh, 2 units above top medial edge of kneecap, on medial edge of vastus medialis m. (on bulge).	ST-12	In a recess at top edge of middle of clavicle, aligned with nipple, 4 units lateral to midline.
PC-3	Inner elbow, on transverse crease, slightly medial to tendon of biceps brachii muscle.	SP-11	Thigh, 6 units above SP-10, at medial side of sartorius m., between SP-10 + 12 (pulse is felt).	ST-13	In a recess at lower edge of middle of clavicle, above and aligned with nipple.
PC-6	Forearm, 2 units above wrist crease, between tendons of long palmar m. and radial flexor m.	SP-12	In inguinal crease, lateral side of femoral artery, 3.5 units lateral to CO-2, where pulse is felt.	ST-17	Chest, in center of nipple. This acupoint is often used as a landmark to locate other acupoints.
SI-5	Ulnar side of wrist, in recess between ulna bone and triquetral bone (wrist joint).	SP-21	Trunk, on midaxillary line, 6 units below armpit, halfway between armpit and free end of 11th rib.	ST-34	Thigh, 2 units above top lateral edge of kneecap, between rectus femoris and vastus lateralis m.
SI-6	With palm facing chest, 0.5 unit proximal wrist, in bony recess on radial side of head of ulna bone.	ST-2	In a recess on top edge of cheekbone, aligned with eye pupil.	ST-35	In a recess below kneecap, lateral to patellar ligament when knee is bent.
SI-8	In recess on flat spot between elbow point (ulna) and medial bony knob of humerus (arm flexed).	ST-3	Directly below eye pupil and ST-2, level with lower edge of nostril.	ST-36	Lower leg, 3 units below ST-35, about 1 unit lateral to crest of tibia bone (shinbone).
SI-11	Flat part of scapula, halfway between left + right edges, 1/3 the distance between ridge and base.	ST-4	Slightly lateral to corner of mouth, directly below ST-3, a faint pulse is felt close below.	TW-3	Back of hand, between 4th and 5th metacarpal bones, in recess proximal base joints of fingers.
SI-17	Directly behind corner of jaw (angle of mandible), recess at anterior edge of sternocleidomastoid m.	ST-5	In a groove-like recess along bottom of jaw bone, on front edge of masseter muscle (pulse is felt).	TW-11	Back of upper arm, 2 units above point of elbow, on triceps brachii tendon.
SP-6	3 units above protruding bone at inner ankle, on rear (posterior) edge of tibia.	ST-7	In front of ear, in recess at lower edge of zygomatic arch, forward of jaw joint.	TW-12	Back of upper arm, at end of lateral head of triceps brachii muscle.
SP-7	6 units above protruding bone at inner ankle, 3 units above SP-6.	ST-9	Side of neck, level with Adam's apple tip, at front edge of sternocleidomastoid m., along carotid a.	TW-17	In recess behind ear lobe, between mastoid process (on skull) and jawbone (mandible).
SP-8	3 units below protruding tibia bone at inner knee, on line joining SP-9 and protruding anklebone.	ST-10	On front edge of sternocleidomastoid muscle, halfway between ST-9 and ST-11.	TW-23	Side of head, in recess at lateral end of eyebrow.

Locating Pressure Points

Pressure points (also called *acupoints*) are usually located in depressions at bones, joints, and muscles. The area affecting each point is usually the size of a dime, but can be as small as a pin head. Some points are easy to locate by simply probing around, since they are very sensitive to pressure. Others are well hidden and require very precise targeting. The angle of attack is often critical. Feel for a slight depression or hollow at each point. This might be a perceived as a slight depression in the bone, or a small space between muscle fibers, tendons, and muscles.

Location Methods

In ancient China, a system using body landmarks and a relative unit of measurement called a *cun*, assisted practitioners in locating points. This system is still in use today. A cun (also called a body inch, unit, or finger unit) varies in length based on the proportion and size of the individual being measured. The length or width of different parts of the fingers are used to make rough estimates of point locations, as shown at right.

Terms Used in This Reference

When describing the locations of pressure points on the human body, it is necessary to use precise anatomical terms to avoid confusion. For example, "above the wrist joint" can refer to either side of the wrist, depending on how the arm is oriented (raised, lowered); whereas, "proximal" is precise, regardless of orientation.

Superior:	Toward the head or upper part of a structure.
Inferior:	Away from head, or toward lower part of a structure.
Anterior:	Nearer to, or at the front of body.
Posterior:	Nearer to, or at the back of body.
Medial:	Nearer to the midline of body, or a structure.
Lateral:	Farther from the midline of body, or a structure.
Proximal:	Nearer to the attachment of an extremity, to trunk or a structure.
Distal:	Farther from the attachment of an extremity, to trunk or a structure.
Superficial:	Toward or on the surface of body.
Deep:	Away from the surface of body.
Unit:	Relative unit of measurement based on use of the fingers.

Abbreviations: (m.) muscle, (n.) nerve, (a.) artery, (v.) vein

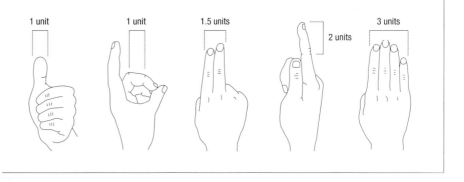

HOLD SUMMARY

This book outlines 159 basic holding techniques used in martial arts. They are summarized at right and shown in subsequent chapters. Basic holding techniques are organized as follows:

10   Wrist Locks
16   Arm Locks
12   Shoulder Locks
18   Finger Locks
12   Leg Locks
12   Nerve Holds
32   Chokes and Head Locks
20   Combinations
17   Defenses Against Chokes
     and Head Locks
10   Defense Against Joint Locks

Technique names are based on commonly used terms. However, within the martial arts there still remains a great deal of variability in term use. Many different terms are often used to represent the same technique. Whenever possible, the clearest or most widely accepted nomenclature is used.

Wrist Locks
1   Bent-Arm Wrist Lock
2   Side Wrist Lock
3   Straight-Arm Wrist Lock
4   Outward Wrist Lock
5   Elevated Wrist Lock
6   Gooseneck Lock
7   Scoop Palm Lock
8   Elevated Palm Lock
9   Figure-4 Palm Lock
10 Inside Palm Lock

Arm Locks
1   Elbow Arm Bar
2   Forearm Arm Bar
3   Inside-Block Arm Bar
4   Descending Elbow Arm Bar
5   Sword Arm Bar
6   Knuckle-Fist Arm Bar
7   Two-Hand Arm Bar
8   Inner-Elbow Arm Bar
9   Wrap-Block Arm Bar
10 Cross Arm Bar
11 Lapel-Assist Arm Bar
12 Inverted Arm Bar
13 Leg Scissor Arm Lock
14 Drop Bent-Arm Lock
15 Outside Twisting Arm Lock
16 Inside Twisting Arm Lock

Shoulder Locks
1   Two-Hand Shoulder Lock
2   Passing Shoulder Lock
3   Outside-Chop Shoulder Lock
4   Inside-Chop Shoulder Lock
5   Outside-Lift Shoulder Lock
6   Inside-Lift Shoulder Lock
7   Scoop Shoulder Lock
8   Driving Shoulder Lock
9   Elbow Hammer Lock
10 Bent-Wrist Hammer Lock
11 Finger Hammer Lock
12 Clapping Shoulder Lock

Finger Locks
1   One-Finger Lock (pinky fulcrum)
2   One-Finger Lock (index fulcrum)
3   One-Finger Lock (thumb fulcrum)
4   Two-Finger Lock (pinky fulcrum)
5   Two-Finger Lock (index fulcrum)
6   Four-Finger Lock (pinky fulcrum)
7   Four-Finger Lock (index fulcrum)
8   Finger Interlock
9   Thumb Lock
10 Pistol Thumb Lock
11 Turning Bent-Thumb Lock
12 Turning Bent-Finger Lock
13 Pressing Bent-Finger Lock
14 Cuticle Bent-Finger Lock
15 Boxing Finger Lock
16 Boxing Thumb Lock
17 Cuticle Finger Lock
18 Fist Finger Lock

Leg Locks
1   Buttock Leg Bar
2   Scissor Leg Bar
3   Two-Hand Leg Bar
4   Twisting Leg Lock + Knee Pin
5   Achilles Ankle Lock
6   Twin Achilles Ankle Lock
7   Single-Leg Crab Lock
8   Twin-Leg Crab Lock
9   Bent-Leg Lock (knee-body lever)
10 Bent-Leg Lock (wrist-body lever)
11 Bent-Leg Lock (inner-thigh lever)
12 Cross-Leg Pin

Chokes + Head Locks

1 Front Naked Choke
2 Rear Naked Choke
3 Front Lapel Choke
4 Rear Lapel Choke
5 Front Double Lapel Choke
6 Rear Double Lapel Choke
7 Rear Cross Choke
8 Half-Nelson Choke
9 Double Sleeve Choke
10 Single Sleeve Choke
11 Arm Trap Choke
12 Rear Interlock Choke
13 Front Interlock Choke
14 Arm Scissor Choke
15 Arm Brace Choke
16 Thrust Choke
17 Knuckle Choke
18 Index Knuckle Choke
19 Thumb-Hand Choke
20 Spear-Hand Choke
21 Tiger-Mouth Choke
22 Pincer-Hand Choke
23 Knife-Foot Choke
24 Knee Choke
25 Leg Interlock Choke
26 Leg Scissor Choke
27 Full Nelson 1 (palms)
28 Full Nelson 2 (Knife Hands)
29 Full Nelson 3 (compress)
30 Twisting Neck Lock
31 Scooping Neck Lock
32 Smothering Neck Lock

Nerve Holds

1 Hair-Pull Hold
2 Hair-Knuckle Hold
3 Lip Hold
4 Double Lip Hold
5 Mouth Hold
6 Ear Hold
7 Clavicle Hold
8 Armpit Hold
9 Biceps Hold
10 Inner-Elbow Hold
11 Testicle Hold
12 Ankle Hold

Pinning Holds

Pinning holds are finishing techniques that are usually an integral part of a series of techniques. Therefore, pins are not covered in a separate chapter, but integrated into the holding techniques found throughout this book, since this is the context in which they are used.

Combinations

There are innumerable possibilities for linking holds to other holds or throws. Twenty typical combinations and transitions are covered in a later chapter.

Defense Against Chokes + Head Locks

Seventeen typical defenses and counterholds are covered in a later chapter.

Defense Against Joint Locks

Ten typical defenses and counterholds are covered in a later chapter.

Wrist locks are holds in which force is primarily applied to the wrist joint. From here it is often transferred to other joints, such as the elbow and shoulder, depending upon the specific hold. Many wrist locks can also be executed using finger holds to assist the technique. Wrist locks generally lead to throws or takedowns, and usually finish with the opponent on the ground, safely under control. Some wrist locks can also be used to restrain an attacker in a standing position. Many wrist locks can be applied with either one or two

WRIST LOCKS

hands, depending on your skill, strength, and the size of your opponent. This chapter outlines ten wrist locks commonly used in Hapkido and other martial arts. The first several pages will describe seven basic forms of stress used in virtually all wrist locks, followed by a quick overview of the ten holds, to help you to understand their fundamental qualities and inherent relationships to each other. Subsequent pages then show each hold, in detail, being executed in a typical self-defense situation. Many other self-defense possibilities also exist.

Basic Stress Motions Used in Wrist Locks

Before learning various forms of holds, it is important to understand the specific anatomical qualities of the joints you are attacking. By examining the basic limitations of the wrist joint, we can better understand the type of force that must be applied to damage it. Generally, there are about seven basic stressful motions that are used in virtually all wrist holds, in varying degrees, to apply destructive force to the joint. These seven motions are shown below and on the next page, using typical wrist lock techniques to demonstrate the type of force that is applied. Since these forms of stress are very destructive, avoid forceful or overly repetitive training, and use wrist flexibility exercises to reduce the likelihood of injury. A typical stretching exercise is shown in the far-right photo of each entry.

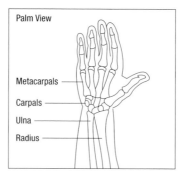

Palm View

Metacarpals
Carpals
Ulna
Radius

Flexibility and Conditioning
When practicing joint locks, flexibility exercises should be done at the start of a training session. This limbers up the joints and over time increases your range of motion, thereby reducing the likelihood of injuries. Practicing these exercises also gives you further practice using the same grips and motions you will use when applying these holds to someone else.

Forward Bend
The wrist is locked forward (the palm-side of the hand is leveraged toward the forearm). The wrist is anatomically weak in this direction and pain is intense. Flexibility, range of motion, and tolerance to pain varies widely by individual. Stocky individuals tend to be less flexible. A *Gooseneck Lock* is a typical hold using this form of stress.

Flexibility Exercise
Grip your L wrist at waist level, with your L wrist straight and your palms facing down: the thumb and middle finger wrap the joint just below (distal) the protruding bones at your wrist; your index finger is extended. Raise your hands to chest level, as you bend your L hand forward by pressing the back of your L hand with your R palm, to lock the joint. Repeat 6–10 times.

Side Bend
The wrist is locked sideways (the pinky-side of the hand is leveraged toward the ulna-side of the forearm). The joint must be precisely aligned to create pain. A *Side Wrist Lock* is a typical hold using this leverage. Leveraging sideways in the opposite direction (toward thumb-side) is ineffective except for a few techniques, as the wrist is strong in this direction.

Flexibility Exercise
Grip your L hand at chest level, with your L wrist straight and your L palm facing forward: your smallest finger wraps the joint just below (distal) the protruding ulna bone at your wrist; the base of the R thumb presses the base of the L index finger. Bend the L hand sideways, pressing its edge toward the edge of the L forearm, to lock the joint. Repeat 6–10 times.

Back Bend
The wrist is locked backwards (the back of the hand is leveraged toward the back of the forearm). The wrist is fairly strong in this direction; however, the tendons in the forearm and hand are very susceptible to damage from stretching. It is usually necessary to stretch the fingers at the same time to generate pain. A *Palm Lock* is a typical hold using this form of stress.

Flexibility Exercise
Grip four fingers of the L hand (exclude the thumb), at chest level, with your L wrist straight and your L palm facing you: your R thumb is against the base joints of the fingers. Bend the L hand and fingers backward and downward (palm up), by pressing down with your R fingers and lifting with your R thumb. This stretches tendons and locks the wrist and fingers. Repeat 6–10 times.

Inward Straight-Twist

The hand is rotated inward with the wrist straight. The elbow can be either bent or straight, depending on the specific hold to be applied. If the elbow is straight, pain is usually rapidly transmitted to the elbow and shoulder. An *Elevated Wrist Lock* (arm bent) and *an Inside Twisting Arm Lock* (arm straight) are typical holds using this form of stress.

Flexibility Exercise

Grip the L hand at waist or chest level, with your L wrist straight and your arms extended away from your body: your R thumb grips the edge of the L palm; your R fingers press the base of the L thumb. You can also grip by reversing the roles of your R thumb and fingers (i.e., R thumb presses L thumb). Twist the L hand inward to lock the wrist and arm. Repeat 6–10 times.

Inward Bend + Twist

The hand is rotated inward with the wrist bent forward. This motion combines the first form of stress (*forward bend*) with a turning motion. This produces complex force in several directions, also transmitting pain to the elbow and shoulder. A *Bent-Arm Wrist Lock* is a common hold using this form of stress. This stress is also used in many arm and shoulder locks.

Flexibility Exercise

Grip the L hand at waist level, with your wrist and arm extended as shown in the photo for the previous exercise. The R thumb grips the L wrist (pinky-side) at HT-7 or SI-5; the R fingers grip the L lower-thumb. Bend the L hand fully forward as you twist it inward. At the same time, rotate the hand upward in a circular motion, toward your chest, locking the wrist. Repeat 6–10 times.

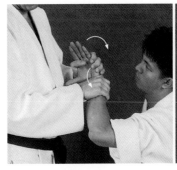

Outward Straight-Twist

The hand is rotated outward with the wrist straight. The elbow can be either bent or straight, depending on the specific hold to be applied. When the elbow is straight, pain is rapidly transmitted to the elbow and shoulder. An *Outward Wrist Lock* (with the wrist straight) and an *Outside Twisting Arm Lock* are typical holds employing this form of stress.

Flexibility Exercise

Grip the L hand at waist or chest level, with your L wrist straight and your arms extended away from your body: your R thumb presses between the 4th and 5th knuckles at TW-3; your R fingers grip the edge of the L palm, with your 4th or 5th finger pressing LU-9 (thumb-side of wrist joint). Twist the L hand outward to lock the wrist and arm. Repeat 6–10 times.

Outward Bend + Twist

The hand is rotated outward with the wrist bent forward. This motion combines the first form of stress (*forward bend*) with a turning motion. This produces complex force in several directions, also transmitting pain to the elbow and shoulder. An *Outward Wrist Lock* (with the wrist bent) is a typical example of a hold using this form of stress.

Flexibility Exercise

Grip the L hand at face level, with your L wrist straight and your elbows close to your body: your R thumb presses between the 4th and 5th knuckles at TW-3; your R fingers grip the edge of the L palm, with your 4th or 5th finger pressing LU-9 (thumb-side of wrist joint). Bend the L hand fully forward as you twist it outward and pull it down to chest level. Repeat 6–10 times.

1. Bent-Arm Wrist Lock

This is a common hold found in many martial arts. The hold is applied by turning the opponent's hand inward, with the wrist and elbow bent ideally about 90°. There are many different methods of gripping, all of which basically direct force in the same manner. When applying the hold, one hand turns the attacker's hand toward their body, the second hand pulls down and inward at the wrist, toward your body. Focusing force at the SI-5 acupoint is very important for efficiency. If you are gripping the wrist, you can press the inner base-joint of your index finger into SI-5 (see drawings below) to assist the hold. When applying this hold, you may stand directly in front of the opponent, or off to the side (about 45°). Regardless of where you stand, or the degree the opponent's arm is bent, keep the held hand pointing toward the vertical midline of the opponent's body. It is not necessary to grip forcefully if force is properly directed. For greater strength, plant the held hand on your chest and use your body weight.

2. Side Wrist Lock

This is similar to the previous hold, except the opponent's arm is extended, with the elbow either slightly flexed or locked straight. Your little finger is seated against the wrist joint. When applying force, keep the opponent's hand pointing toward the vertical midline of their body, or angled directly in line with the forearm (when the elbow is fully extended). This hold is often used while stepping backward, or as a transition from a *Bent-Arm Wrist Lock* if an opponent straightens their arm. This hold is applied using one or two hands, although two hands provide better control and grip security.

3. Straight-Arm Wrist Lock

With the opponent's arm extended, lock the wrist by pressing the palm toward the forearm, as you rotate the hand. Rotation is crucial, since it forces the shoulder down. Push with your thumb(s) at the back of the hand, between the knuckles at TW-3 and M-UE-24, as you pull with your fingers at the inner wrist. The hand is held above the attacker's shoulder, but no higher than your chest. This hold must be well executed to be effective. Since holds 1, 2, and 3 are closely related, transitions between these holds are common when an opponent struggles or attempts to counter.

4. Outward Wrist Locks

Turn the opponent's hand outward, as you twist and press down to lock the wrist and elbow. There are numerous methods of gripping—all directing force similarly. Push with your thumb(s) between the back knuckles (TW-3 and M-UE-24), and pull with your fingers at the inner wrist (LU-9). When the elbow is against the body, the joints lock faster. You can execute this hold the wrist and elbow bent (most common), wrist bent and elbow straight, wrist straight and elbow bent, or wrist and elbow straight.

5. Elevated Wrist Lock

The wrist is twisted inward with the hand held high and vertical. Keep the opponent on their toes, unbalanced and stepping around in a circle. You may also lock the pinky finger backward, and press into the base joint of the thumb, to assist the hold.

6. Gooseneck Locks

The wrist is *bent forward,* with the fingers pointing up or down. Trap the opponent's bent-elbow between your arm and body. Lock the wrist by pressing their palm toward the forearm, using one or both hands. Place your fingers on the back of the hand, with the thumbs against the inner wrist. This hold can be used as an escorting technique, or to lower an opponent to the ground.

7. Scoop Palm Lock

The trapped wrist and fingers are *bent backward* by elevating the elbow and pulling it toward your chest. Grip the elbow with one or both hands. The opponent's fingers are trapped on your chest as a result of the pressure you are applying at their elbow.

8–10 Palm Locks

The wrist and fingers are *bent backward,* by gripping the fingers. The hold can be directed in a variety of directions, based on the variation used. The Elevated Palm Lock (8) is often used to throw an attacker into an obstacle or another attacker. The Figure-4 Palm Lock (9) is commonly used to counter a one-hand push or a straight palm-strike. The Inside Palm Lock can be adapted to a variety of situations, and is sometimes entered by stepping under the attacker's arm. This hold also works well as a transition to, or from, an Elevated Wrist Lock.

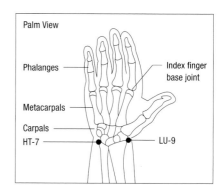

1. Bent-Arm Wrist Lock

2. Side Wrist Lock

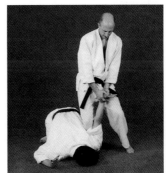
3. Straight-Arm Wrist Lock

4. Outward Wrist Lock (bent wrist)

5. Elevated Wrist Lock

6. Gooseneck Lock

7. Scoop Palm Lock

8. Elevated Palm Lock

9. Figure-4 Palm Lock

10. Inside Palm Lock

1. Bent-Arm Wrist Lock

Attacker grabs your opposite wrist. Form a Live-Hand (A). Trap attacker's hand on your wrist, with your L hand. Pull back and lead inward (fake) (B). Push forward and circle your R hand outward and over, grabbing their wrist in the "V" between your thumb and index finger (C). Lock the wrist toward the forearm, as you twist their hand forward. Pull down and back at their wrist with your other hand. Use your upper-body weight and lean to assist. Drop to one knee and pin (D–E).

Important Points

There are more than 19 variations in methods of gripping (see author's book, *Hapkido: Traditions, Philosophy, Technique*). Regardless of how you grip, keep the held-hand pointing toward the vertical midline of attacker's body. Lock attacker's wrist sideways and forward as you twist their hand, focusing force at SI-5. Ideally, the elbow and wrist are bent about 90°. If attacker straightens their arm, shift to a Side Wrist Lock (see next technique), Straight-Arm Wrist Lock (see technique 3), or arm bar (see Elbow Arm Bar and Forearm Arm Bar, in *Arm Locks* chapter).

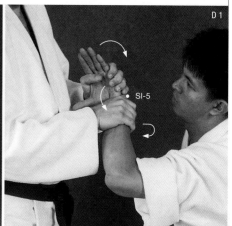

2. Side Wrist Lock

Attacker grabs your lapel or pushes you with one hand (A). Pivot right and trap their hand on your chest, with both hands: your L fingers grip the edge of their palm; your L thumb presses the base joint of thumb; your R hand grips the wrist, hand, or fingers (B). Pivot left, step back with your L foot, and pull attacker's arm straight, as you rotate their hand until the little finger faces up (C). Step back with your R foot. Pull inward at the wrist with your little fingers, as you press the edge of their hand forward toward the edge of their forearm, locking the wrist (D). Drop to one knee and pin (E).

Important Points

Turn and lean your upper body to power the hold. Clamp the attacker's hand tightly between your palms and keep their hand pressed firmly to your chest. Keep stepping backward and pulling forcefully, since this positions attacker's wrist and keeps it locked. It also protects you against kicks or hand strikes, and unbalances the attacker. Lean slightly forward to assist the lock (D). If attacker bends their arm, shift to a Bent-Arm Wrist Lock (see previous hold). If they rotate their arm, shift to an arm bar.

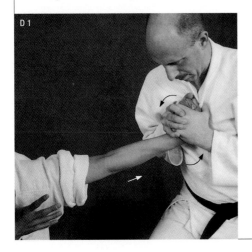

3. Straight-Arm Wrist Lock

Attacker grabs your opposite wrist. Form a Live-Hand (A). Trap attacker's hand on your wrist with your L hand. Lead inward (fake). Circle your R hand outward and up, as you step laterally and pull their arm straight (B). Lock the wrist forward as you twist the arm (C). Force a fall and pin by kneeling on the shoulder. Lock the elbow on your inner leg, while locking the wrist (D). If they bend their arm or turn away to relieve pain, shift to a Bent-Wrist Hammer Lock (D1).

Important Points

By itself, this isn't a strong hold, unless your technique is good. Your thumbs push between the knuckles at TW-3 and M-UE-24, as you pull with your fingers and press attacker's palm toward their forearm. Twist the hand as you lock the joint, to force the shoulder down. Don't hold attacker's hand higher than your shoulders, since you are weaker and the hold is more easily countered. To keep the arm from bending, stay to the side. If you lose control, shift to an Elbow Arm Bar or Forearm Arm Bar (see *Arm Locks* chapter).

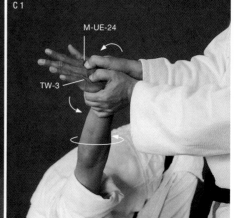

4. Outward Wrist Lock

Attacker grabs your opposite wrist. Form a Live-Hand (A). Lead outward (fake). Circle your hand inward and up. Reach under and grip attacker's hand, twisting it outward: your thumb presses TW-3, your fingers pull the edge of the palm (B). Break their thumb by driving your R wrist clockwise around the hand (C), finishing with your Knife Hand on the back of their hand (D). Push and twist their hand down to lock the wrist. Step forward, pivot, and force a fall (E).

Important Points

Twist attacker's wrist in a tight circular motion. Do not use large movements. This hold can also be executed by stepping forward with your L foot, past attacker's left side. Stepping forward adds power to the wrist lock and protects your groin from strikes. There are many methods of gripping. Photo D2 shows an alternate two-hand grip commonly used. You can also execute this hold with one hand only, although this requires sensitivity and a good understanding of leverage principles.

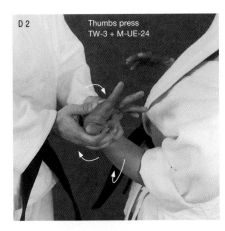

Thumbs press
TW-3 + M-UE-24

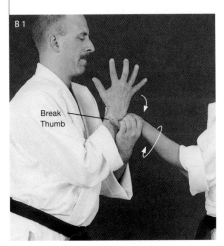

Break Thumb

TW-3

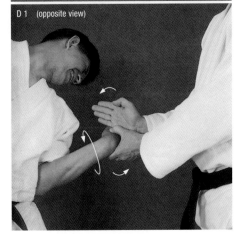

D 1 (opposite view)

A

B

C

D

5. Elevated Wrist Lock

Attacker grabs your cross wrist (A). Grip their wrist with your R hand (underhand); grip their hand with your L hand. Step back with your R foot and pull to your hip (B). Step forward with your R foot, twist their wrist inward, and elevate their elbow (C). Pass under the arm, pivot 180°, and lock the wrist (D) (fingers pull at edge of palm, thumb presses LI-4 at web of thumb). Keep attacker on their toes, stepping in a circle. If you wish to throw, drop to one knee as you pull and twist their hand forward and down (E).

Important Points

Your initial back-step and pull causes the attacker to either step toward you or pull back. In either case, this sets up your entry under their arm. Lock the wrist (D) using either grip shown at right (D1, D2). Both grips use similar *complex* motions: vertical lift, horizontal twist, and slight angular leverage (keeps elbow up). Keep opponent's hand vertical and lock their wrist by controlling their *hand.* Twisting the wrist alone provides poor leverage. If attacker drops their elbow to escape, make a transition to a Gooseneck Lock (see next technique).

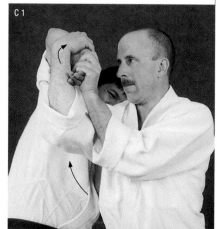

C1

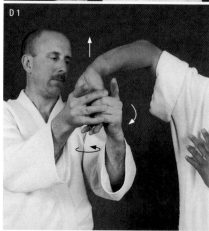

D1

E

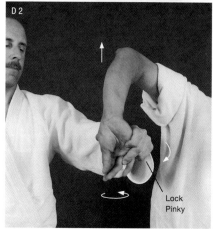

D2

Lock Pinky

6. Gooseneck Lock

Attacker grabs your opposite wrist. Form a Live-Hand (A). Grab attacker's wrist with your held-hand, as you chop their inner elbow with your Ridge Hand (B), forcing the arm to bend. Begin locking their wrist with one hand, as your other hand hooks their elbow, pulling it into your arm-body trap (C). Wrap the back of attacker's hand with two hands (thumbs at their wrist). Lock their wrist forward, pressing their palm toward their forearm (D). Drop to one knee and pin, if needed (E).

Ridge Hand

Important Points

This hold can be used either as an escorting technique or to lower an attacker to the ground. Although the wrist lock is strong and painful, you may be vulnerable to hand strikes or kicks if you remain standing. If you sense a threat, quickly take your opponent to the ground by increasing wrist pressure (and pain), as you drop to one knee (E). Pain alone will often discourage further resistance. You can also break the wrist if justified. If attacker lifts their elbow to escape, shift to an Elevated Wrist Lock (see previous technique).

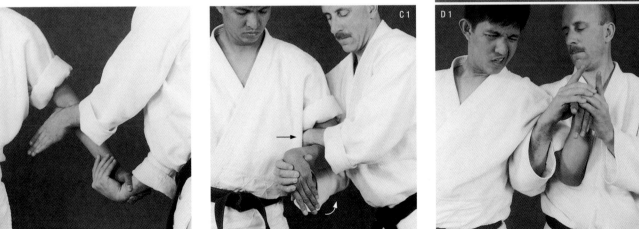

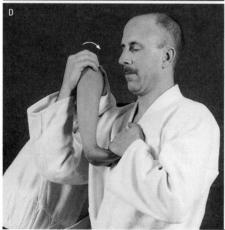

7. Scoop Palm Lock

Attacker pushes you with one hand. Step back and absorb the push (A). Step 45° forward with your L foot. Pin attacker's fingers on your chest, with your L hand. Grip their elbow with your R hand (thumb at HT-3 or PC-3) (B) and scoop it upward and back toward you (C). This bends the fingers and wrist backward, stretching tendons and locking joints (C). You can also apply this hold by pulling the elbow with both hands.

Important Points

Focus force at opponent's fingertips, not their palm. Once the hold is applied, attacker's wrist will remain trapped on your chest due to the pressure you are applying at their elbow. This is the reason you can also apply this hold with both hands on their elbow. Use either hold (one- or two-handed) to briefly restrain an attacker, or to damage their wrist or fingers. A transition to a Finger Hammer Lock is described in the *Combinations* chapter.

8. Elevated Palm Lock

From a relaxed stance (A), step forward with your L foot to opponent's outside. Grab their R hand with your L hand. Twist their palm up and lock their wrist backward (B). Your palm is against the back of their hand. Grip four fingers with your R hand. Lock the fingers and wrist by levering the fingertips toward their forearm. Your palm pushes the fingers, your fingers pull the base joints. Step past with your R foot, forcing a Back Fall (C–D).

Important Points

This hold is used to unbalance an opponent backward, forcing a Back Fall. If it is executed quickly and forcefully, the fingers will break and the wrist tendons will be torn. Focus force at opponent's fingertips, not their palm. Pressing their palm prevents you from effectively stretching the wrist tendons. If you wish to control opponent while standing: grip the two smallest fingers and apply a finger lock, using your index finger as fulcrum.

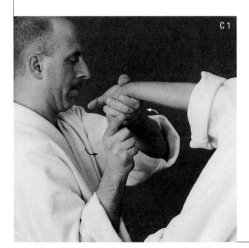

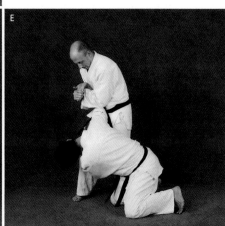

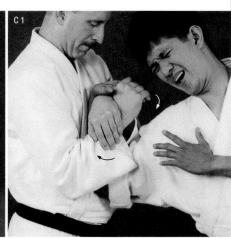

9. Figure-4 Palm Lock

Attacker pushes you with one hand. Step back, absorb the push (A). Bring your L hand down onto attacker's wrist (B); trap it on your chest. At the same time, bring your R hand up behind attacker's hand, grab four fingers, and bend them back to lock the wrist and fingers. Grab your R wrist with your L hand and pinch your elbows together to trap the arm (C). Lock the fingers and wrist, as you twist attacker's hand and pivot toward their inside (D), forcing them to drop (E).

Important Points
This hold is simple and strong, once you master the entry. Keep your hands tight to your body, trapping attacker's bent-arm from the elbow up. Don't let their elbow swing freely or the hold may fail. Use your body weight and shoulder-turn to create power. Moderate force creates significant pain. Stress is transmitted to the fingers, wrist, elbow, and shoulder. To avoid injuries, apply slowly. You can also reverse the role of your hands.

10. Inside Palm Lock

Attacker applies a bear hug, pinning your arms (A). Thrust your Live-Hands forward and your buttocks backward (B). As attacker's hands separate, grip their cross-hand and twist it inward. Your thumb presses their thumb-knuckle, as your fingers pull the edge of their hand (C). Turn inward 180° and pass under the arm: your L foot pivots, your R foot steps (D). Twist with both hands until the palm faces up. Pull the fingers down and back, locking the fingers and wrist. Drop to your R knee to force attacker to the ground (E).

Important Points

When breaking the bear hug (B), exhale to increase power and focus your energy. You can also release attacker's hands by gouging nerves. When applying the lock (E), attacker's fingers should point toward their face. Grip all four fingers, with your thumbs on the back of their hand (E1). Use your R elbow to control their elbow position. Don't point your index fingers (Live-Hands), or they may be grabbed or bitten. This entry can also be used to apply an Elevated Wrist Lock (see technique 5).

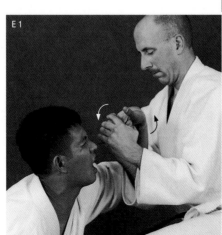

Arm locks, the largest category of holds in the martial arts, are techniques in which force is primarily applied to the elbow joint and the surrounding tendons and ligaments of the arm. Sometimes stress is also transferred to other joints, such as the shoulder and wrist, depending upon the specific hold and the degree of force. Many arm locks also incorporate wrist locks to strengthen the hold. Most arm locks generally lead to takedowns, and usually finish with the opponent on the ground, safely under control, although some holds can

ARM LOCKS

also be used to restrain an attacker in a standing position. This chapter outlines sixteen basic arm locks commonly used in Hapkido and other martial arts. The first several pages will describe basic principles, followed by a quick overview of the sixteen holds, to help you to understand their fundamental qualities and inherent relationships to each other. Subsequent pages then show each hold, in detail, being executed in a typical self-defense situation. These holds are very adaptable and can be used in many other scenarios as well.

BASIC CONCEPTS

There are three basic categories of arm locks, which are characterized by the manner in which force is applied to the arm:

• Arm Bars
• Bent-Arm Locks
• Twisting Arm Locks

In arm bars, the arm is straight and the elbow is locked or hyperextended. In bent-arm locks, the arm is bent and nerves at the inner elbow are attacked. In twisting arm locks the entire arm is twisted, which also stresses the wrist and shoulder. When taken as a whole, these three categories encompass hundreds of different techniques and variations.

Arm Bars

Arm bars are used extensively in many martial arts and are the largest and most varied category of arm locks. The arm is fully extended, with the elbow joint locked. Arm bars primarily attack the elbow, causing pain or dislocating the joint, although some also incorporate locks to the wrist and shoulder.

Force is usually applied at two points, in opposing directions: 1) the back of the elbow joint, and 2) the wrist. The primary focus is the elbow, an inch or two above the joint, at TW-10 or TW-11 (the site of several major nerves and the triceps tendon). TW-11 is the ideal point, since it is very sensitive to pressure, particularly when using bony surfaces to apply the hold. As you apply force to the elbow, the opponent's wrist is either moved in the opposite direction or held in a stable position. Although arm bars can be applied by gripping the wrist, it is usually considered more effective to combine them with a wrist lock, since this creates additional pain without breaking the elbow. When comparing arm bars in different martial arts, one finds that energy-oriented martial arts tend to focus more on blending, unbalancing, and pressure point attacks to assist the hold; whereas, power-oriented arts tend to emphasize force, pronounced use of body weight, strong grips, and a more direct transfer of leverage forces.

Variable Factors for Arm Bars

Most arm bars can be applied in limitless ways, depending upon the situation. They are generally varied based on these factors:

Body Position

Holds are applied from an opponent's outside or inside, or from above and below. This applies to standing or ground positions.

Methods of Holding Wrist

Secure the wrist area by: using a *wrist lock*, *grabbing the wrist* with one or both hands, or *trapping the wrist* using your hands, wrist, elbow, upper arm, shoulder, neck, back, legs, or body.

Direction of Force

Force applied to the elbow is used to move an opponent in specific directions. Upward or lateral force is often used to make a transition into other holds.

Downward	(to move to the ground or pin)
Upward	(to escort; moving on tips of toes)
Lateral	(to move; or pin against the wall)

Methods of Attacking the Elbow

Apply force to the elbow using any part of your body. When targeting the nerve at TW-11, use protruding bones to press this point. Common methods are:

Wrist	(protruding bone at each side)
Forearm	(edge of radius or ulna bone)
Inner Elbow	(protruding humerus bone)
Elbow Point	(protruding ulna bone)
Armpit	(clamping tight to your body)
Shoulder	(muscle or protruding bone)
Knife Hand	(protruding 5th finger base joint)
Knuckles	(point of thumb or finger joints)
Palm	(base joints of fingers)
Knee	(edge of tibia bone)
Lower Leg	(edge of tibia bone)
Foot	(blade-of-foot or heel)

Finishing the Hold

Finish holds by forcing an opponent to the knees, or flat onto the stomach (safest). A standing opponent leaves one vulnerable to counters, and is only recommended when you are sure of your superiority and safety.

Bent-Arm Locks

In these techniques, you will force the opponent's elbow to close tightly around the protruding bones of your wrist or ankle. Then you will twist your bone against their inner elbow. This causes extreme pain at the biceps tendon and median nerve. This hold is similar to closing a door with an object jammed into the hinge. With sufficient force, the elbow may dislocate. Bent-Arm Locks are often used to unbalance and throw, or force a submission when ground fighting.

Twisting Arm Locks

These techniques emphasize "twisting the arm" to stress the wrist, elbow and shoulder. The elbow may be either bent or extended. These holds are typically applied by clamping the wrist with both hands, then twisting it as you pass under the opponent's arm and pivot 90–180°. Exercise caution: these holds can be very destructive to tendons and ligaments, and will result in tears and dislocations if forcefully applied. When training, reduce arm stress by allowing the opponent's arm to slip in your grip, as you twist and pivot.

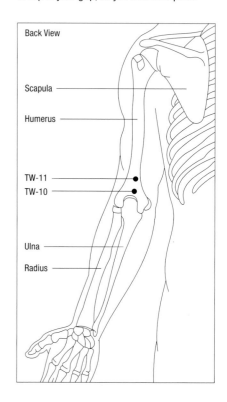

Back View
Scapula
Humerus
TW-11
TW-10
Ulna
Radius

Types of Arm Locks

Arm Bars (arm straight, elbow locked)

Bent-Arm Locks (arm bent, nerves being attacked)

Twisting Arm Locks (arm twisted)

Variable Factors for Arm Bars

Body Position

A. Outside
B. Inside
C. Above
D. Below

Direction of Force

A. Focus Points
B. Downward Force
C. Upward Force
D. Lateral Force

Finishes

A. Standing
B. Drop to One Knee
C. Sit-Out (body drop)
D. Pin (wall or ground)

1. Elbow Arm Bar

Grip the opponent's wrist and hand. Lock their wrist and twist their arm, as you lock their elbow with the bony part of your inner elbow. Lift their wrist upward as you press downward on their elbow. This hold can also be applied without locking the wrist (just grip it), or by using your armpit to press and lock the elbow. The Elbow Arm Bar is one of the strongest forms of arm bar, since you can use your entire body weight to assist if needed.

2. Forearm Arm Bar

This is similar to the previous technique, except you will use the bony part of your wrist (pinky-side) to press downward on the opponent's elbow at TW-11 (triceps tendon). When properly done, this hold can produce significant pain, without damaging the joint.

3. Inside-Block Arm Bar

This hold is similar to the previous hold, except you will trap the opponent's wrist instead of gripping it. The Inside-Block Arm Bar is normally used to engage a punch that is too fast to grab, or during fast transitions in which it is not prudent or possible to attempt a more secure grip. Trap the opponent's wrist in your inner elbow (clamp tight). Lift their wrist as you lock their elbow by pressing the bony part of your wrist (pinky-side) into the triceps tendon at TW-11.

4. Descending Elbow Arm Bar

Grip the opponent's wrist and twist their arm. Lift their wrist upward as you lock their elbow by pressing the back of your elbow downward into the triceps tendon at TW-11.

5. Sword Arm Bar

Twist the opponent's hand or wrist inward to position their arm. Swing your extended arm downward, in the manner of a sword cut, driving the side of your elbow into the triceps tendon at TW-11. Depending on the length of an opponent's arm, relative to your arm, it may be necessary to press their elbow with other surfaces, such as your upper arm (use the edge of the humerus bone) or forearm (use the edge of the ulna bone).

6. Knuckle-Fist Arm Bar

Grip the opponent's wrist and twist their arm. Form a fist with your other hand. Lift their wrist upward as you lock their elbow by pressing your second set of knuckles downward into the triceps tendon at TW-11. Bend your wrist, using a rolling circular motion to drive your knuckles into sensitive nerves at the elbow. When properly done, this hold can produce significant pain without damaging the elbow joint, since it permits pinpoint targeting of TW-11.

7. Two-Hand Arm Bar

The opponent's wrist is braced on either your shoulder, upper arm, or inner elbow. Lock the opponent's elbow by pulling it downward with both hands. Numerous grips are possible.

8. Inner-Elbow Arm Bar

Grip the opponent's wrist with both hands and pull it to your waist. Lock their elbow by pivoting your body, as you drive your upper arm or inner elbow into their elbow, just above (proximal) their joint.

9. Wrap-Block Arm Bar

This hold is applied using one arm only. Tightly wrap the opponent's elbow with your arm, trapping their arm in your armpit. Lock their elbow by driving your forearm (radius bone) into the triceps tendon at TW-11. Based on the orientation of their elbow, this hold can be used to keep an opponent standing, direct them sideways, or force them to the ground.

10. Cross Arm Bar

Grip both wrists. Twist opponent's arms and cross their elbows, entangling them. Use the forearm of one of their arms (which is bent), to lock the elbow of their other arm (which is straight), pressing just above their joint.

11. Lapel-Assist Arm Bar

Grip the opponent's wrist with one hand. Grip high on their lapel with your other hand, planting your inner elbow just above their elbow joint. Lock their elbow by pushing their wrist downward, as you lift your inner elbow by extending your arm and wrist upward.

12. Inverted Arm Bar

Grip the opponent's wrist with one hand. Tightly wrap the opponent's elbow with your other arm. Lock their elbow by pushing their wrist downward, as you drive your forearm (radius bone) upward into the triceps tendon at TW-11. This hold is normally used to restrain an opponent while standing or break the arm. It can also lead to a takedown if the arm is twisted to reposition the elbow.

13. Leg Scissor Arm Bar

This hold is an example of an arm bar applied with your legs. There are numerous other possibilities as well. Grip the opponent's wrist with one or both hands. Swing your leg over their arm. Lock their elbow by scissoring your legs as you pivot your hips, forcing the wrist and elbow to move in opposing directions.

14. Drop Bent-Arm Lock

Plant your wrist in the opponent's inner elbow. Use your other hand or your shoulder, to drive their wrist toward their shoulder, forcing their elbow to close tightly around your wrist. When your wrist is trapped tightly in their elbow, twist the protruding bones of your wrist against nerves at their inner elbow (very painful). Drive downward to unbalance and force a fall. This hold is also used as a transition, when an opponent counters your arm bar by bending their elbow.

15. Outside Twisting Arm Lock

Grip the opponent's wrist and twist their arm. Continue to twist the arm as you step under it and pivot 180–360°, stressing the joints, ligaments, and tendons of the wrist, arm, and shoulder. When stepping under the arm, you will pass from outside the arm, to its inside. This hold usually leads to serious injuries.

16. Inside Twisting Arm Lock

Grip the opponent's wrist and twist their arm. Continue to twist the arm as you step under it and pivot 180–360°, stressing the joints, ligaments, and tendons of the wrist, arm, and shoulder. When stepping under the arm, you will pass from inside the arm, to its outside. This hold usually leads to serious injuries.

1. Elbow Arm Bar

2. Forearm Arm Bar

3. Inside-Block Arm Bar

4. Descending Elbow Arm Bar

5. Sword Arm Bar

6. Knuckle-Fist Arm Bar

7. Two-Hand Arm Bar

8. Inner-Elbow Arm Bar

9. Wrap-Block Arm Bar

10. Cross Arm Bar

11. Lapel-Assist Arm Bar

12. Inverted Arm Bar

13. Leg Scissor Arm Lock

14. Drop Bent-Arm Lock

15. Outside Twisting Arm Lock

16. Inside Twisting Arm Lock

1. Elbow Arm Bar

Attacker grabs your opposite wrist. Form a Live-Hand (A). Trap attacker's hand on your wrist with your L hand. Lead inward (fake). Circle your R hand outward and up, grabbing their wrist in the "V" between your thumb and fingers (B). Step across, pull their hand to your chest, and twist it until the elbow points up (C). Lock the wrist and elbow: bend and twist the hand; drive your inner elbow down into the joint, as you lift the wrist (D). Drop to one knee and pin (E). You can also pin by shifting the locked-elbow to your armpit and dropping your hips to the ground (F).

Important Points

This is a very strong hold, since you can use your body weight to assist. There are many variations. The most common involve locking the elbow with your elbow or armpit, as you lock the wrist (D1). Controlling the hand and locking the wrist is essential, since this turns attacker's elbow, lowers their shoulder, and creates pain. Step forcefully across for power (C). Always take attacker directly to the ground, to avoid counters.

F (optional transition to Armpit Arm Bar)

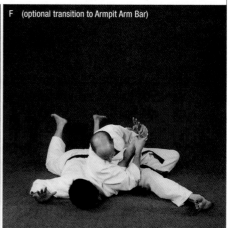

2. Forearm Arm Bar

Attacker grabs your opposite wrist. Form a Live-Hand (A). Lead inward (fake). Circle your hand outward and up. Twist attacker's hand with your L hand, until their elbow points up. Drive your R wrist forward, to break their thumb and release their hold (B). Step across. Lock the wrist and pull up, as you press your R wrist down into TW-11, locking the elbow (C–D). If desired, you can use your thigh to reduce free-play (D1). Pin by dropping to one knee. Place their arm flat on the ground and maintain your hold (E). You can also pin by kneeling on TW-11 (see next technique).

Important Points

You must rotate attacker's arm until their elbow points up. Your left hand assists by twisting their hand. Your right wrist assists by driving into attacker's elbow—up, over, and down. Begin by pushing their elbow at the *side of the joint,* and finish *above the back of the joint*. This rotates and locks their elbow, even if the elbow is bent or facing sideways. There are many variations on this basic hold, and it can be applied to many situations.

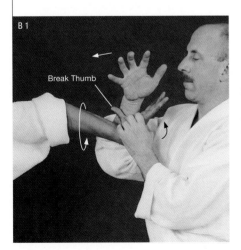

B 1

Break Thumb

D 1

TW-11

3. Inside-Block Arm Bar

Step outside a lead straight strike. Execute a L Inside Block to the elbow at TW-11, as you trap attacker's wrist between your forearm and your upper arm and chest (A–B). This locks or breaks their elbow in a single action, without grabbing. Press the elbow downward with your forearm as you lift their wrist, unbalancing attacker to their right front-corner (C). Force a fall. Pin by continuing to press TW-11 (D), or by kneeling on this point (E). Kneeling provides a strong, painful hold.

Important Points
This technique does not require you to secure a grip, making it useful against fast strikers. Execute *quickly* and *forcefully*. Direct your block slightly upward, to assure that you lock the joint. Otherwise the elbow may bend. Drive your forearm up, over, and down. Clamp tight when you trap the wrist between your chest and forearm. If attacker counters by bending their arm, quickly make a transition to a *Drop Bent-Arm Lock* (see technique 14).

Trap

TW-11

4. Descending Elbow Arm Bar

Attacker grabs your opposite wrist. Form a Live-Hand (A). Lead inward (fake). Circle your hand outward and over attacker's wrist in a tight circular motion, gripping their wrist in the "V" between your thumb and index finger. Twist their arm and pull laterally as you execute an Inside Elbow Strike to their chin (B). Keep twisting attacker's arm. Lock their elbow by driving your elbow down into TW-11 (above the joint), as you lift their wrist (C). Drop to one knee and pin (D).

Important Points

The crucial part is getting attacker's elbow properly positioned for the arm bar (back of the elbow pointing up). If the arm is under-rotated, drive your elbow more toward your chest. If elbow is pointing down, wrap the arm and lock the elbow in the opposite direction (C2). If an attacker keeps reorienting their elbow, you can apply an arm bar in any direction, by barring with either your wrist, upper arm, armpit, or chest.

Elbow Strike

5. Sword Arm Bar

Attacker grabs cloth at your shoulder (A). Reach across and trap their hand: your fingers grip the edge of their palm; your thumb presses the base joint of their thumb (B). Twist attacker's hand as you step back and pivot 90°, circling your extended arm up (C). Attacker's elbow and palm now face up. Swing your arm down like a sword, planting your elbow at TW-11 (D). Drive downward to lock or break the elbow (E).

Important Points

It is crucial to *twist* attacker's hand, *pivot* forcefully, and *step* back. These actions rotate and straighten attacker's arm, so their elbow is positioned for the arm bar. As your arm crosses attacker's elbow, it resembles a very narrow "X". While applying the arm bar, you can also attack nerves in the neck (D1) by driving your fingertips into ST-9, ST-10, or CO-22; and your thumb into TW-17 or SI-17. Many other pressure point possibilities exist.

A

6. Knuckle-Fist Arm Bar

Attacker chokes you with one arm (A). Grip their wrist and elbow. Pull their wrist down with your L hand (your palm faces out), lift their elbow with your R palm, and pivot 90°. Lock their shoulder as you duck under their arm (B). Step away as you pull their arm straight. Lock the elbow by lifting their wrist, as you press your Knuckle Fist down into TW-11 (C). Pull attacker off-balance to their right front-corner, force a fall, and pin (D).

Knuckle Fist

Important Points

When applying a Knuckle-Fist Arm Bar, you will press into attacker's triceps tendon at TW-11, using your second set of knuckles. Rolling your wrist slightly as you apply pressure (D1), will increase pain and help isolate the nerve. Accuracy is very important. When properly applied, this hold produces extreme pain, making it very easy to control your opponent. You can also lock their elbow by using your Knife Hand, forearm, or elbow.

Knife Hand

B

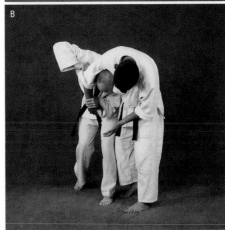

C

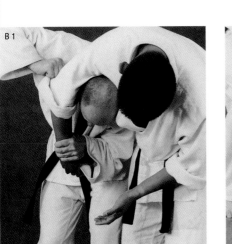

B 1

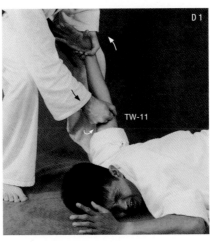

D 1

TW-11

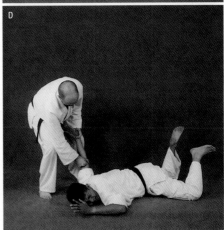

D

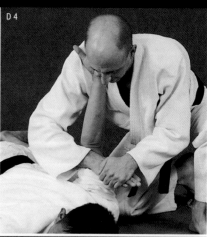

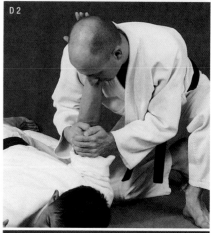

7. Two-Hand Arm Bar

Attacker grabs your collar with their arm bent (A). Clamp your hands on both *sides* of their bent-elbow (B); your fingers can be either interlocked (D1) or overlapped (D2). Step 45° forward, lift, and pivot as you rotate attacker's bent-arm until their elbow points up (C). Step backward and pull down to straighten their arm and lock their elbow (D). Scrunch your shoulder and tilt your head, to trap their wrist (D1). Drop to one knee and pin (E).

Important Points

The entry shown is often used to counter a grappler, who secures a rear-collar hold (usually to pull your head down to set up a throw). Their arm will be bent for strength and to prevent arm bars. You must clamp the elbow *very tight*, and it must be *bent*. Otherwise, it is difficult to overcome attacker's natural resistance. When turning attacker's arm, pivot your body under their elbow, and lift it using your shoulders, hips, and legs for power. Two-Hand Arm Bars can also be applied using other grips and entries. In D3 and D4, you will use the bony edge of your wrist or forearm to press TW-11.

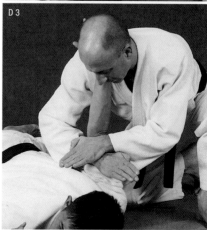

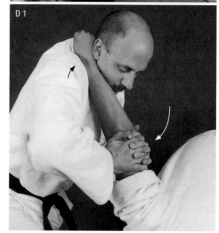

8. Inner-Elbow Arm Bar

Attacker grabs your cross-wrist (A). Grab their wrist with your held-hand, and cross-step forward with your R foot. Pull their wrist to your R hip, as your R hand reaches under their arm and grabs your own hand to assist (B). Lock their elbow by turning your torso horizontally downward as you step across (C). Attacker's wrist is trapped at your R hip; their elbow is locked against your upper arm. As attacker circles forward, block their far leg (D) and force a fall. A skilled attacker will initiate a Flip Side Fall (E) or a shoulder roll, to prevent serious injuries. An unskilled attacker will fall forward face-down.

Important Points

This technique is fast and deceptive. When applying the elbow lock, use your body weight, hip turn, shoulder turn, and leg thrust to generate power. You can also lock attacker's elbow with your shoulder or inner elbow. If an attacker twists their elbow to counter, the arm bar can be redirected in any direction, including upward (lift your elbow, pull their wrist down). Dropping your body weight rapidly downward is the most destructive form of takedown.

9. Wrap-Block Arm Bar

Step inside a lead strike, block outward (A–B), and wrap attacker's elbow tightly, trapping their wrist against your back (C). Use your inner elbow or upper arm to apply lateral pressure to the elbow joint. Pivot to your left to lock the elbow (D). Redirect the arm bar downward by leaning your upper body forward as you maintain constant pressure. Force a fall to attacker's left front-corner. Drop to one knee and pin (E).

Important Points

You must move quickly to trap the arm tightly against your back. Any slack or hesitation will allow attacker to twist or withdraw their arm, and you will be left with nothing. As you direct the arm bar sideways and down, bend forward and drop to one knee, pinning attacker face down. If attacker counters your entry by dropping and bending their elbow, execute a *Scoop Shoulder Lock* (see *Shoulder Locks* chapter). The Wrap-Block Arm Bar can also be used to counter a hip throw by applying the hold as attacker reaches around your lower back.

A

B

C

D

10. Cross Arm Bar

Attacker grabs both of your wrists. Form Live-Hands (A). Circle both hands clockwise left (B). Grip both wrists and continue twisting clockwise, as you step across with your R foot and pivot 180°. Attacker's arms are now crossed, with their L forearm locking their R elbow at TW-11 (C). Pass under the arms. Keep locking the joints as you turn both arms (D). Drive your R hand downward as you pull your L hand upward, forcing a Flip Side Fall (E–F).

Important Points

If attacker pulls their L hand free, shift to a Forearm Arm Bar, applying it to their R arm (see technique 2). Instead of flipping your attacker (F), you can also finish this hold with a takedown and pin (G–H). To execute this variation, apply steps A–D as previously described. Then, drive your R hand down, pull your L hand up, and pull attacker toward their left front-corner to unbalance them and force a fall (G). Drop to one knee and pin, as you continue to lock the elbow (H).

G

E

H

D 1

TW-11

F

11. Lapel-Assist Arm Bar

Attacker grabs your belt, palm up (A). Cross-step forward with your L foot. Grip their wrist as your R hand passes under their arm (B). Grip high on the lapel and plant your *bent* inner elbow behind their elbow. Lock their elbow by extending your R arm and wrist upward, as you push their wrist down (C). Pivot 180°, plant your R knee on their knee. Redirect the arm bar downward by turning your R arm (D). Extend your R knee into their knee and force a fall. A skilled opponent will initiate a Flip Side Fall to save their arm (E).

Important Points

Grip as high on the lapel as possible. If you can grip the collar, you will also be able to apply a Lapel Choke, as you lock the elbow. Make sure your inner elbow is pressed tight against attacker's elbow, *before* you extend your arm. Use *wrist action* to assist leverage, driving your knuckles into nerves below the clavicle at KI-27 or ST-13 (C1). You can also swing your R leg back into attacker's ankle, knee, or thigh, sweeping them off their feet (essentially a throwing technique).

Knuckle at KI-27 or ST-13

12. Inverted Arm Bar

Attacker grabs your opposite wrist. Form a Live-Hand (A). Grab attacker's wrist with your L hand, step forward, and lever your R hand free, as you lock or break the elbow with your R upper arm (B). Execute two Outside Elbow Strikes to the ribs (C) and head (D). Rake TW-11 with your thumb-knuckle as you wrap the arm and lock the elbow (E). This hold is often taught as an escorting technique. However, if an opponent remains standing, the hold is much less secure, since you can be struck

with their free hand or kicked. To execute a takedown, maintain the arm bar as you redirect it downward by twisting attacker's wrist and bending forward (F). Lift their wrist, as you lock their elbow across your chest. Force a fall by dropping to your knees, or by trapping their leg from the front as you force a Front Fall (G). Pin the attacker in a prone position. You can maintain the same arm bar throughout the takedown (G1), or shift to an Armpit Arm Bar on the ground (an example is shown in technique 1, earlier in this chapter).

Important Points

Raking the triceps tendon above the elbow (TW-11), momentarily relaxes the arm and allows you to apply the arm bar. Pull the wrist down and drive your forearm upward, pressing your protruding inner wrist into TW-11. Use pronounced *wrist action* to increase the range-of-motion of your wrist. Keep the opponent on their tiptoes and moving, or take them immediately to ground. If you wish to keep attacker standing and you are losing control, direct them into a wall or harmful obstacle, or into another opponent.

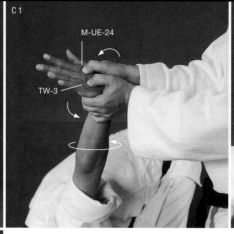

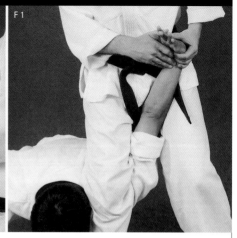

13. Leg Scissor Arm Lock

Attacker grabs your opposite wrist. Form a Live-Hand (A). Trap attacker's hand on your wrist with your L hand. Lead inward (fake). Circle your R hand outward and up, as you step laterally and pull their arm straight (B). Lock the wrist forward as you twist the arm (C). As attacker bends over, swing your leg up and over their arm (D), planting your foot on the other side of attacker's arm. Their held-arm is now trapped between your legs (E). Lock attacker's elbow and shoulder by scissoring your legs together, as you twist your hips (F). Use the back of your L knee and your R upper thigh to apply leverage, as you continue pulling back on the locked wrist (F1). If you wish to pin attacker face-down, sit down on their elbow or shoulder, applying a shoulder lock or Buttock Arm Bar Pin (G). When swinging your leg over their arm (D), you can either wrap the arm gently, or bring your leg forcefully downward to break the elbow. In either case, plant the back of your knee or calf just above the elbow, as you drive downward. There are many other methods of entering this hold.

A

14. Drop Bent-Arm Lock

Step forward to attacker's outside, as you parry a lead straight punch, with your L hand (A–B). At the same time, strike down into the head of the biceps and inner elbow, with your R Knife Hand or Outer Wrist. Push downward as you turn your wrist against the inner elbow (painful), trapping attacker's bent-arm on your chest (C). Pull them toward their rear-corner to throw. As they fall, grab the wrist. Pull the wrist upward and back toward your upper thigh, as you lock the elbow on your knee (D).

Important Points
This technique does not require you to secure grips with your hands, making it useful against fast strikers. Execute the hold with speed and power as you charge inward, committing your entire body. Pull the elbow inward and drive downward, as you push your chest forward. This forces the elbow to close *tightly* around your wrist, generating intense pain as you twist it. If attacker straightens their arm, quickly shift to an *Inside-Block Arm Bar* (see technique 1).

Knife Hand

Outer Wrist

B

C

C 1

C 2   (opposite view)

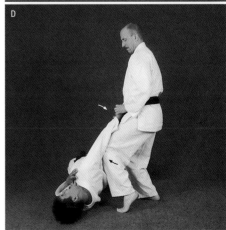

D

NaNARM LOCKS

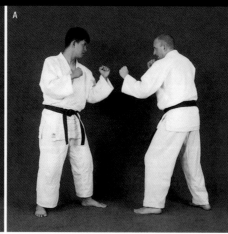

15. Outside Twisting Arm Lock

Step inside a straight or inside circular strike. Parry outward with your R hand (A–B) and grip attacker's wrist. Twist their arm as you pass it downward and up to your left, gripping with both hands (C). Step forward with your R foot (D), pass under their arm, and pivot 180°, twisting and locking the arm (E). Twist and lift their straight-arm, breaking the wrist, elbow, or shoulder (F). A skilled attacker will initiate a Flip Side Fall to save their arm (G).

Important Points
Because this entry is longer than most holds, you must move quickly. Pull forcefully sideways as you step, to unbalance attacker and prevent a rear-hand punch. Lock attacker's elbow with your upper arm as you step under it, to prevent counters. Keep the held-hand low and close to attacker's body as you pull upward (E). This locks the elbow against their belly. If attacker bends their elbow during your entry (C–D), shift to a Passing Shoulder Lock (see *Shoulder Locks* chapter). Both holds use the same basic entry.

16. Inside Twisting Arm Lock

Step outside a straight or outside circular strike. Parry outward with your R hand and grip attacker's wrist (A–B). Twist their arm as you pass it to your left, gripping with both hands (C). Step forward with your L foot (D), step under the arm with your R foot, and pivot 180°, twisting and locking their arm (E). Whip their arm forward and down. A skilled attacker will initiate a fall to save their arm and shoulder from serious injury (F).

Important Points

This hold locks attacker's wrist, arm, and shoulder by step D, causing serious injuries. It can be applied with attacker's arm either bent or straight, and by either passing close to their body or farther away. As you parry the blow, pull attacker toward you and into the hold. Pass the arm down and across in a circular motion. Twist their hand and elevate their elbow as you enter (D). As you pass under the arm, keep their hand twisted in front of your head. During training, allow your partner's wrist to slip in your hands, to avoid damaging their arm as you twist and pivot.

Shoulder locks are holds in which force is primarily applied to the shoulder joint and the surrounding tendons, ligaments, and bones. In some instances, considerable stress is also transferred to the elbow or wrist, depending upon the specific hold and the degree of force. Some shoulder locks also incorporate wrist locks or finger locks to strengthen the hold or assist your entry. Most shoulder locks generally lead to takedowns and pins, and usually finish with the opponent on the ground, safely under control. Some variations can also be

SHOULDER LOCKS

used to restrain an attacker in a standing position. This chapter outlines twelve basic shoulder locks commonly used in Hapkido and other martial arts. The first several pages will describe basic principles, followed by a quick overview of the twelve holds, to help you to understand their fundamental qualities and inherent relationships to each other. Subsequent pages then show each hold, in detail, being executed in a typical self-defense situation. These holding techniques can also be adapted to many other combative situations.

SHOULDER LOCKS

In shoulder locks, force is primarily directed to the shoulder joint, although the elbow and wrist may also be subjected to considerable stress. When forcefully applied, a shoulder lock can cause: a *shoulder dislocation* by forcing the head of the humerus out of the glenoid fossa (see drawing), or a *shoulder separation* (less likely) by tearing ligaments around the acromioclavicular joint, causing the clavicle to separate from its normal alignment with the joint. Both these injuries are very painful, producing obvious joint deformity and limited range of motion.

There are two basic types of shoulder locks: 1) those executed from the side or front, where the arm is forced *backward,* causing an opponent to fall backward (holds 1–7); and 2) those executed from behind, where the arm is forced *forward,* causing an opponent to fall forward (holds 8–12). During struggles, opponents will often inadvertently lead themselves into shoulder locks, in an effort to escape other holds, such as wrist locks.

When applying shoulder locks, it is important to realize that flexibility in the shoulder joint varies widely by individual. Always practice slowly and gently until you are familiar with your partner's range-of-motion. Be aware that accidental dislocations during training are not uncommon. Be very careful when practicing with someone who has had a previous shoulder dislocation, since subsequent dislocations can often occur quite easily.

1–6 Front Shoulder Locks

Six common types of Front Shoulder Locks are shown in this chapter. They are characterized by different methods of gripping and entering, although they all basically direct force to the shoulder in a similar manner. To apply, lift up and inward at the elbow and drive down at the wrist, forcing the arm backward. When the arm is bent about 90° (elbow is away from their body) the technique is powerful, and the shoulder can dislocate easily (anterior dislocation). If an opponent's arm is tightly bent and close to their body, they will have more power to resist.

There are numerous variations in methods of gripping, all applying the same form of stress. The specific grip used is based on the type of entry (e.g., grab, being grabbed, blocking a strike, etc.). When grabbing the elbow, you can also seize pressure points to assist the hold (e.g., LU-5, HT-3, LI-11). Sometimes Front Shoulder Locks also incorporate wrist locks to increase efficiency and reduce the necessity for muscle power. If you do not hold the wrist, a Front Shoulder Lock can be easily countered by applying the same hold in reverse. If an opponent fully elevates their elbow (pointing straight up), which is common, pull straight down to effect a takedown. Otherwise, lower your body as you apply the hold (e.g., drop to one knee). This allows you to control an opponent without dislocating their shoulder. If you remain standing during certain shoulder locks, the shoulder will often dislocate.

7. Scoop Shoulder Lock

The shoulder and elbow are stressed in the same direction as a *Front Shoulder Lock.* Clamp the wrist in your armpit. Sweep the opponent's bent-elbow upward by driving your thumb-knuckles or wrist into the side of their bent-elbow at LI-11. You can also lift the elbow with your inner elbow (less efficient). The range of motion this hold produces is shorter than other Front Shoulder Locks; consequently, your technique must be good.

8. Driving Shoulder Lock

Drive the opponent's bent-elbow forward and downward as you pull the wrist upward. The opponent's arm is bent about 90° throughout the technique. This hold typically causes an opponent to fall forward, or 45° forward toward the held-arm. Transitions to a *Hammer Lock* or *Forearm Arm Bar* are common when an opponent attempts to struggle or counter.

9–11 Hammer Locks

The arm is placed behind the back. Lock the shoulder by lifting up at the wrist and driving the elbow inward and back. Hammer Locks can be used to restrain an opponent while standing, or to make a transition to a ground pin (opponent is seated or prone). There are five basic variations: The *Elbow Hammer Lock* is applied by lifting your elbow (to lift the trapped wrist) as you drive down with your Knife Hand, pulling your opponent's elbow toward your body and forcing a front fall. Hammer locks can also be used to restrain an opponent while they are standing upright.

Clavicle
Ligaments
Ligaments
Glenoid Fossa
Humerus

View from front of shoulder

Traditional hammer locks were often applied by pressing the upper arm (left); modern versions press the elbow (right).

An older method of applying an Elbow Hammer Lock involves driving the blade of your hand against the upper arm, instead of the inner elbow (see photos on previous page). This hold is generally weak and easily countered, although many martial artists continue to use it. The *Bent-Wrist Hammer Lock* uses a wrist lock to assist the hold, which makes it very painful and effective. *Finger Hammer Locks* use painful finger locks to assist entering and locking the shoulder.

12. Clapping Shoulder Lock

This unusual hold is usually only used to counter a belt-grab. It is basically a two-hand Driving Shoulder Lock (see # 8) that shifts to a Hammer Lock (see #9) as you pin the opponent. Drive the opponent's elbow with the blades of both hands and force a fall to their front-corner. If needed, step over the arm to tighten the lock (see photo). Exercise caution, since this will likely cause a dislocation, unless the opponent is very flexible.

Shoulder Lock Pins

If you take an opponent to the ground, most shoulder locks lead into pins, without changing grips. Often you will also try to lock the wrist or elbow or apply a choke at the same time. There are many possibilities. Common pinning techniques are incorporated into most of the techniques shown on the following pages. Against multiple attackers, pins are impractical. In these cases, throw quickly and move on to the next attacker.

1. Two-Hand Shoulder Lock

2. Passing Shoulder Lock

3. Outside-Chop Shoulder Lock

4. Inside-Chop Shoulder Lock

5. Outside-Lift Shoulder Lock

6. Inside-Lift Shoulder Lock

7. Scoop Shoulder Lock

8. Driving Shoulder Lock

9. Elbow Hammer Lock

10. Bent-Wrist Hammer Lock

11. Finger Hammer Lock

12. Clapping Shoulder Lock

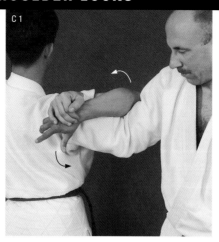

Ridge Hand

1. Two-Hand Shoulder Lock

Attacker delivers a high straight strike or descending strike (Hammer Fist is shown). Step forward to the outside. Execute a L Rising Block with your forearm to attacker's wrist (A–B). Hit upward to their inner elbow with your R Ridge Hand, bending their arm. Grip their wrist with both hands. Pull downward as you lift your R elbow, locking their shoulder (C). Force a Back Fall, unbalancing attacker toward their rear or right rear-corner (D). To pin, kneel on attacker's shoulder and pull their wrist laterally to lock their arm and shoulder (E). At the same time, press your R thigh laterally into their upper arm to assist.

Important Points

This is mostly used against descending strikes. You must block early and step past attacker as you strike their inner elbow. Try to grip their *wrist and hand* (not the forearm), or they can apply the same hold on you. Two grip variations are shown (C1, C2). When pinning (E), pull the wrist sideways with the elbow bent and pointing up. You can also use the pins shown for techniques 2 and 6.

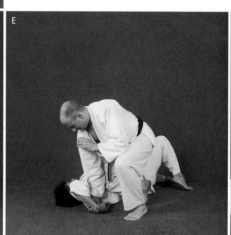

2. Passing Shoulder Lock

Attacker grabs your cross-wrist. Form a Live-Hand (A). Lead inward (fake). Circle your held-hand outward (right), up, and over, gripping attacker's wrist (overhand grip). Twist their arm and step 45° forward, as your L hand grips the elbow (thumb at LU-5, middle finger at HT-3 or SI-8 (B). Step under their arm with your L foot and pivot 180°, twisting their bent-arm, to lock the shoulder (C). Pull attacker's wrist down, while pushing their elbow up and over (D), forcing a Back Fall. Press their elbow down to the ground, as you pull their wrist under their shoulder (E), trapping it underneath their arm. Block or strike with your R hand as needed (F).

Important Points

As you step in, drive attacker's elbow up as you pull their wrist down. This locks the shoulder *before* you pass under the arm, hindering counters. When locking the shoulder (D1), try to use a wrist lock to assist (force their palm toward their forearm). Do not grip above their wrist (on forearm), since they will be stronger. Keep your head tucked behind their arm for protection (D). Drive your body forward and down for power.

HT-3 or SI-8

LU-5

Ridge Hand

Inner Wrist

3. Outside-Chop Shoulder Lock

Attacker delivers a high straight strike or descending strike (Hammer Fist shown). Step forward. Execute a R Rising Block with your forearm to attacker's wrist (A–B). Chop their inner elbow with your L Ridge Hand, bending their arm (C). Grip their wrist with your R hand and push down, as you lift their elbow with your L forearm, locking their shoulder and wrist (D). Drive your elbow into the jaw (D1). Force a fall. Maintain the hold. Pull attacker's wrist laterally to lock their arm and shoulder, as you apply a choke with your elbow by pressing the throat at ST-9 or ST-10 (E).

Important Points

As you enter, keep your head tucked behind your block for protection. You can also apply this hold without gripping, by pressing with your R wrist, directly off your block. Strike forcefully to the inner elbow at the head of the biceps with your Ridge Hand or Inner Wrist. Drop your head and bend forward as you apply the hold. Drop to one knee, throwing attacker to their rear or right rear-corner. Two common grip variations are shown (D1, D2).

4. Inside-Chop Shoulder Lock

This is like the previous technique (#3), only you will reverse the roles of your hands. Step forward. Execute a L Rising Block with your forearm to attacker's wrist (A–B). Chop their inner elbow with your R Ridge Hand, bending their arm. Grip their wrist with your L hand and push down, as you lift their elbow with your R forearm, locking their shoulder and wrist (C). Drive your elbow into the jaw. Force a fall (D). Maintain the hold. Pull attacker's wrist laterally to lock their arm and shoulder, as you apply a choke with your elbow by pressing the throat at ST-9 or ST-10 (E).

Important Points

Two grip variations are shown (D1, D2). As you enter, try to use your elbow to hit the chin or face. You can also slip your hand past the elbow, and grasp your own wrist (D2). This hold may feel stronger, but both work equally well. If attacker attempts to lift their elbow during step E, press down on it with your R shoulder (their forearm is vertical). The *Important Points* outlined for technique 3 also apply to this hold, and vice versa.

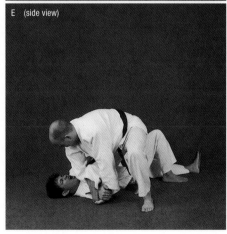

E   (side view)

5. Outside-Lift Shoulder Lock

Attacker delivers a straight or outside circular strike. Step outside the blow. Block with both palms to attacker's wrist and elbow, then grip both (A–B). Gouge pressure points on the elbow and bend the arm, circling attacker's hand toward their head (C). Step in with your R foot and pivot anywhere from 180° to 360°. Bend the wrist and lock it outward. Lock the shoulder by lifting their elbow inward, as you twist and push down on their hand (D). Maintain the shoulder lock and pin. Release one hand and strike if needed (E).

Important Points

When gripping the elbow, gouge LU-5 with your middle finger, and HT-3 with your thumb (if your hand is too small, press LU-5). When pivoting, your arms will cross as you lock the shoulder (D). During your pivot bring your hips close to attacker's hips: this adds power and makes it easier to unbalance them. If you wish to throw without dislocating the shoulder, you must lower your body while maintaining the hold. Only a skilled opponent will initiate a Flip Side Fall to save their arm (D1).

Press LU-5 and HT-3 at elbow

6. Inside-Lift Shoulder Lock

Attacker delivers a straight or inside circular strike (a hook punch is shown). Step inside. Execute a L Knife Hand Block to their wrist, hitting nerves if possible (A–B). Grip their wrist with your L hand. As attacker pulls away (bending their arm), grip their elbow with your R hand, pressing LU-5 and HT-3. Scoop attacker's elbow up and push their wrist down to lock their shoulder (D). Force a Back Fall. Pin by kneeling on their ribs, and the side of their neck or jaw. Pull their wrist upward and toward your right-rear to lock their elbow against your R thigh (E).

Important Points

This hold works best when an attacker strikes with their arm bent, or pulls away. Do not drop your R arm when reaching for their elbow. Keep your elbow high (B) until the last moment or you can be hit by a left punch. As you lift their elbow, gouge LU-5 with your middle finger, and HT-3 with your thumb. Exercise caution when kneeling on the neck or jaw, since serious injuries can occur. Be ready to quickly stand up if you lose control.

Alternate Pins (E1, E2)

Photos E1 and E2 show alternate methods of pinning an opponent. To apply E1, press attacker's elbow down to the ground with your R palm, as you pull their wrist under their shoulder with your L hand. This traps their hand underneath their upper arm. You can now release your grip on their wrist and maintain the hold with one hand (E1). Use your free hand to block or strike as needed. This pin was also shown in technique 2.
To apply E2, pull attacker's arm straight and press their wrist (palm-down) against the ground. Use one or both hands. Kneel on their elbow at TW-11 to pin the arm and lock the shoulder and elbow (painful). Be sure to keep attacker's arm pressed against their head, with their arm fully extended.

Generally, you can shift into any of the three pins shown (E, E1, E2), as attacker falls to the ground. Base your choice on the dynamics of the situation. For example: if you can keep attacker's arm fully bent, shift into E1; if attacker forces their arm straight, shift into E2. There are also numerous other variations.

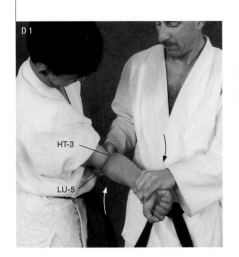

HT-3
LU-5

E 1 (alternate pin)

E 2 (alternate pin)

7. Scoop Shoulder Lock

Attacker's delivers a hook punch with their arm bent. From inside the blow, block outward to their inner elbow or wrist, using a Knife Hand (A–B). Wrap and scoop attacker's bent-elbow inward and up, as you trap their wrist in your armpit (C). As you scoop their arm, drive your forearm, wrist, or thumb-knuckles against their bent-elbow. Lift up to lock or dislocate the shoulder (D). Step back and drop to one knee, to force a fall (E).

Important Points

This works well against bent-arm punches, such as a hook or uppercut, particularly those thrown to middle targets. Keep your other hand up, to prevent attacker from grabbing your R hand or striking your face, with their free hand (C). To take attacker down without dislocating their shoulder, step back and drop to one knee. If force is justified, clamp tight as you sit-out into a Back Shoulder Roll (devastating). You can also throw by sweeping their L foot with your R foot. If attacker straightens their arm during step C, shift to a Wrap-Block Arm Bar (see *Arm Locks* chapter).

8. Driving Shoulder Lock

Attacker grabs your lapel (A). Trap their hand on your chest, with your L hand: L fingers grip the edge of their palm; L thumb presses the base joint of their thumb (B). Step forward with the R foot. Twist attacker's hand, as you lift their elbow with your Knife Hand or Live-Hand (C). Cross-step behind your R foot with your L foot and pivot 180°. In a circular motion, drive attacker's bent-elbow up, over, and down to lock the shoulder (D). Push their knuckles with your L palm to lock their wrist. Force a Front Fall and pin (E). Alternate pin: kneel on their upper arm as you push their wrist forward (F).

Knife Hand

Important Points

This hold often flows naturally into either a Hammer Lock or Forearm Arm Bar, based on how attacker struggles. If they straighten their arm (or you pull it straight), you have an arm bar. If they turn away to relieve pain, their arm will be behind their back (easy transition to a Hammer Lock). This hold is also used when an opponent counters an arm bar by bending their elbow. A shoulder roll can provide an escape, if done early.

Live Hand

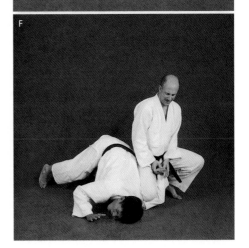

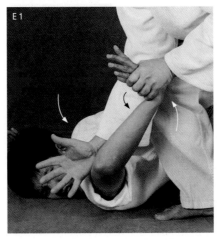

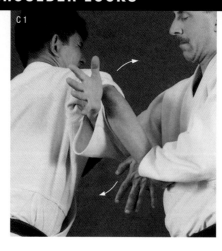

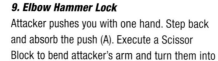

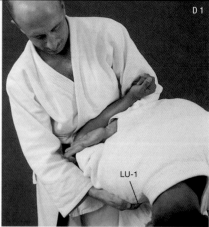

LU-1

9. Elbow Hammer Lock

Attacker pushes you with one hand. Step back and absorb the push (A). Execute a Scissor Block to bend attacker's arm and turn them into the hold: your R wrist hits up and back, into the elbow at HT-3; your L wrist hits down and forward, into the wrist at LI-5 (B–C). Pivot and drive your L wrist up. Trap their wrist in your inner elbow and lift, as you plant your Knife Hand in their inner elbow and drive down. The shoulder is now locked (D). At this point, you can either force a fall or remain standing. To throw, keep pivoting and levering the shoulder as you force attacker to fall toward their right side or right front-corner. Force them flat onto their belly and sit on their lower spine (E), as you continue locking the shoulder. To restrain an attacker while standing, you must keep them from bending over to initiate counters. To force attacker upright, press LU-1 (D1) or their throat. Then, you can either: continue pressing LU-1 (E1); press the base of their throat at CO-22 (E2); grip their left lapel and choke them with your wrist (E3); pull hair; or press other sensitive pressure points, such as the clavicle at ST-12, or the base of the neck at ST-11.

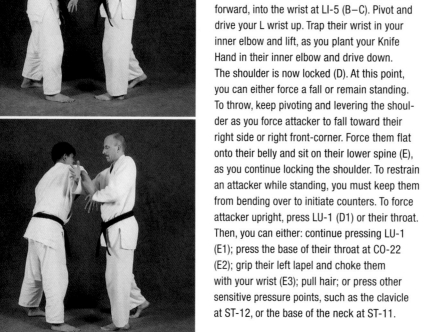

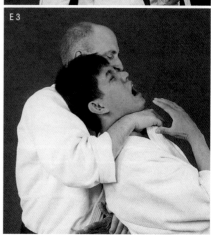

10. Bent-Wrist Hammer Lock

Attacker grips your opposite wrist. Form a Live-Hand (A). Lead inward (fake), then outward. Grip attacker's wrist with your R hand and pull laterally (overhand grip is shown, but underhand also works). Grip their elbow, pressing your L thumb into PC-3 or HT-3 (B). Lift their elbow as you pull their wrist down. Step under the arm with your L foot and pivot 180° (C). Your R palm begins pressing at the back of the hand to lock the wrist forward, as you lock their arm behind their back. Your L grip has shifted: your L thumb presses HT-3, your L middle finger presses LI-11 (D1). This is painful and reduces resistance. Lock the shoulder by lifting the wrist and driving the elbow inward and back (D). Pivot to your left, unbalance attacker toward their left side or left front-corner, and force them to fall to their knees or belly. Maintain your hold (E). For greater security, force attacker flat on their belly and sit on their lower spine. During your entry (C), the shoulder should be partially locked and the arm well-controlled, before you step under the arm. This discourages counters.

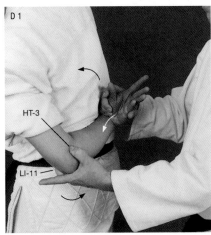

11. Finger Hammer Lock

Attacker pushes you with their R hand. Step back and absorb the push (A). Trap their hand against your chest with your R hand (your palm faces your chest). Wrap attacker's two smallest fingers, placing your smallest finger on the base joints. Lock their fingers backward and slightly sideways. Grip their elbow with your L thumb at LU-5, and middle finger at HT-3 (B). In a circular motion, pull their elbow up as you guide the finger lock behind their back (C). Trap their elbow between your elbow and body. Lift the finger lock to lock the shoulder (D).

Important Points
This hold works quickly, requires very little strength, and creates intense pain. You can grab any finger you like, although the two smallest create the most pain with the least effort. Lock the fingers as soon as you grip (B). Keep circular leverage tight and focused. This hold can be used as an escorting technique. You can also use the finger lock to force an attacker directly down to the ground, instead of placing their arm behind their back.

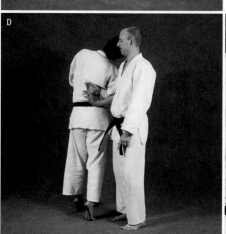

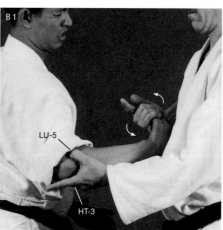

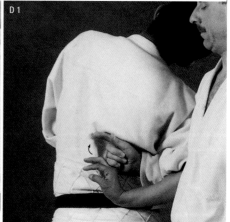

12. Clapping Shoulder Lock

Attacker grabs your belt, palm up (A). Step forward with your L foot, and clap your hands together under their arm (B). Circle both hands outward and up, lifting their elbow at HT-3 with your R wrist (C). Their hand is trapped in your belt. Pivot 180° as you drive their elbow up, over, and down with both Knife Hands, to lock the shoulder (D–E). If their shoulder is *flexible*, step over with your L foot to lock it tighter (F), then sit on their back. Exercise caution, since this stepping motion can easily cause a dislocation. During training omit step F, or release the hold as you step over.

Important Points

This hold is basically a two-hand *Driving Shoulder Lock* (E) that turns into a *Hammer Lock* as you step across (F). It is important to turn your body, step in very close, and use your body weight to drive downward. Exaggerate your shoulder-turn, and pull toward attacker's right front-corner to unbalance them and force a fall. Use your R elbow and hip position to lift their wrist as you apply the lock (E). Think of *cranking the arm*.

Knife Hand

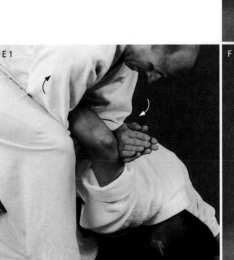

Finger locks are holds in which force is primarily applied to the joints of the fingers. They are one of the most powerful techniques for controlling an opponent's movement. With the proper hold, you can instantly direct a person in any direction—into a wall, into another attacker, to the ground, or bring them to their feet and escort them to another location. Finger locks require very little force and are particularly useful for children or smaller individuals facing larger, more powerful opponents. They can be used during grappling to

FINGER LOCKS

counter a choke or hold, instantly controlling the opponent. The only time finger locks are ineffective is against individuals who cannot feel the pain, such as persons under the influence of drugs. In this situation, you may break the finger and they may still keep fighting. The next few pages provide a quick overview of eighteen finger locks, to help you to understand their essential qualities. Subsequent pages then show eight of the more common locks, in detail, in typical self-defense situations. Numerous other applications exist.

FINGER LOCKS

Finger locks are joint lock holds in which force is first applied to the fingers. From here stress is often transferred to other joints, such as the wrist, elbow, or shoulder. The degree of skill and sensitivity you possess will largely determine the efficiency of these techniques. To grasp someone's finger and break it is not "rocket science." However, to seize a person's finger and control them in a precise, efficient and gentle manner, by *regulating pain*, is a highly developed skill. This requires training, sensitivity, a thorough understanding of hand anatomy, and a good teacher.

While anyone can learn finger locks based on photos and achieve reasonable results, a high level of efficiency requires demonstration, supervision, and extensive practice. While Hapkido contains many sophisticated finger locks, which are the basis of the material in this chapter, the author is particularly indebted to Professor Wally Jay, the renowned Jujutsu pioneer, for sharing many of his unique technical innovations in this area.

Leading and Controlling

When using finger locks to lead an opponent, they will move in the direction you point their palm: if you wish to force them to the ground, point their palm down; if you wish to force them to stand on tiptoes, point their palm up; pointing their palm sideways creates lateral movement. This principle is also used to make transitions into other wrist locks, arm locks, or pins. To turn or redirect their palm, use short rotations of your wrist and hand, maintaining constant pressure. Avoid big looping arm motions as they accomplish nothing.

Transitions to Other Holds

When turning the hand inward, you will transition to inward wrist locks, such as the *Bent-Arm Wrist Lock.* When turning the hand outward, you will transition to an *Outward Wrist Lock.* The strongest control is obtained by grabbing two fingers, since pain is more easily applied (two smallest fingers work best). Four-finger holds are weaker, since an opponent has more strength to resist.

1. One-Finger Lock (pinky fulcrum)

This is the most basic and useful method of applying a finger lock. Wrap the opponent's finger with your smallest finger against their base joint. Pull with your two smallest fingers, while pushing at the fingertip with your palm. Drive their fingertip toward their forearm. This basic grip and wrist-action is also used in many weapon techniques.

2. One-Finger Lock (index fulcrum)

Wrap the opponent's finger with your extended index finger pressed against their base joint. Apply by rotating your hand, as you pull their fingertip toward their forearm. Usually their palm faces up.

3. One-Finger Lock (thumb fulcrum)

Trap the finger between your thumb and the base of your index finger. This hold is used to attack any joint (base, second, or third). Apply by rotating your hand, with your thumb rigidly extended.

4. Two-Finger Lock (pinky fulcrum)

This is the same as the one-finger version (see #1), except you will grab two fingers. The two smallest fingers work best. However, in a fight you will often have to grab whatever you can.

1. *One-Finger Lock (pinky fulcrum)*

2. *One-Finger Lock (index fulcrum)*

3. *One-Finger Lock (thumb fulcrum)*

5. Two-Finger Lock (index fulcrum)

This is the same as the one-finger version (see #2), except you will grab two fingers. When holding the two smallest fingers, you can also direct force sideways by twisting as you apply leverage.

6. Four-Finger Lock (pinky fulcrum)

This is the same as the two-finger version, except you will grab four fingers. Forcefully squeeze the fingers together, clashing the joints. Twist the fingers as you leverage either the base or second joints. Favor the smaller fingers, which are weaker.

7. Four-Finger Lock (index fulcrum)

This is like the two-finger version, except squeeze four fingers together, clashing joints as you twist and lever. Focus force at small fingers if possible.

8. Finger Interlock

Interlock the opponent's two or three smallest fingers between your three largest fingers (index, middle, ring). Rotate their palm up and leverage one or more fingers back toward their forearm. Do not wrap larger fingers, since they can perform the same technique on you. This is an opposite-hand technique, although cross-hand is also possible.

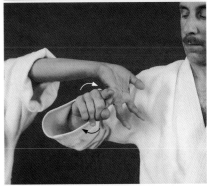

4. Two-Finger Lock (pinky fulcrum)

5. Two-Finger Lock (index fulcrum)

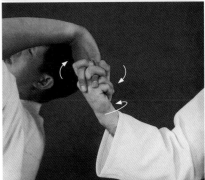

6. Four-Finger Lock (pinky fulcrum, twist and lever)

7. Four-Finger Lock (index fulcrum)

8. Finger Interlock

9. Thumb Lock

This is basically a *One-Finger Lock* applied to the thumb. Leverage the opponent's thumb toward the edge of their forearm. Try to keep their wrist relatively straight; if it bends, step away and pull.

10. Pistol Thumb Lock

Wrap your fingers around the thumb and wrist, squeezing the thumb toward the wrist.

11. Turning Bent-Thumb Lock

Twist the bent-thumb outward and down with your thumb. Wrap your index and middle fingers under the base joint; pull inward and up. The wrist and thumb lock outward.

12. Turning Bent-Finger Lock

Wrap your index finger around one of the opponent's fingers (middle or ring works best). Plant your middle finger behind their base joint. Press sideways against their bent-fingertip with your thumb; pull inward with your index finger. The finger and wrist lock outward.

13. Pressing Bent-Finger Lock

Use the same grip as the previous hold. Push down and back on the opponent's fingertip, forcing the finger closed. Focus stress at the third joint (not the second, a common mistake). You may also lock the base joint by lifting with your middle finger.

14. Cuticle Bent-Finger Lock

This is the same as the previous hold, except press into the cuticle with your fingernail (very painful).

15. Boxing Finger Lock

This is similar to the previous two holds, except your bent index finger is placed below the held-finger. It is possible to create greater stress, since your index finger is no longer in the way.

16. Boxing Thumb Lock

Force the thumb to bend beyond its normal limit by pressing the tip toward the base joint. Push with the heel of your hand. Pull with the fingers.

17. Cuticle Finger Lock

Trap the extended finger between the index and middle fingers of your clenched hand. Press your thumbnail into the cuticle. Drive your index finger down against the joint. Pull up with the middle finger.

18. Fist Finger Lock

Wrap your hand over the attacker's fist, leaving free space. Place your fingertips against their fingertips. Squeeze inward, stressing the third set of joints.

9. Thumb Lock

10. Pistol Thumb Lock

11. Turning Bent-Thumb Lock

12. Turning Bent-Finger Lock

13. Pressing Bent-Finger Lock

14. Cuticle Bent-Finger Lock

15. Boxing Finger Lock

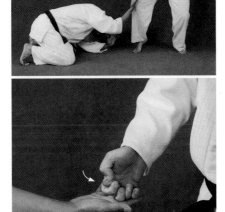

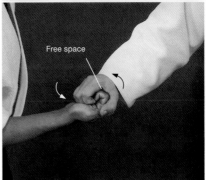

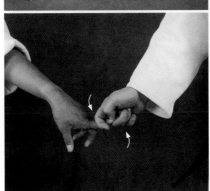

Free space

16. Boxing Thumb Lock

17. Cuticle Finger Lock

18. Fist Finger Lock

A. One-Finger Lock (pinky fulcrum)

Attacker pokes you with their R index finger (A). Quickly wrap their index finger with your R hand, placing your smallest finger on their base joint. Pull with your two smallest fingers, while pushing their fingertip with your palm. Drive their fingertip toward their forearm (B). This generates immediate pain and forces attacker to drop (C). Step backward as you continue locking their finger, forcing attacker to lie flat on their belly (D).

Important Points

This hold is fast, requires little strength, and creates intense pain. Try to grab attacker's finger with your cross-hand. This puts you on their outside, making it harder for them to hit you with their free hand, or kick. Avoid large motions; use tight circular leverage. If the attacker's fingers are very flexible, press upward against their palm to tighten the finger lock. You can do this with your thigh, knee, or free hand. Persons influenced by narcotics may not react to pain, even if their finger breaks. In this case, shift to other techniques.

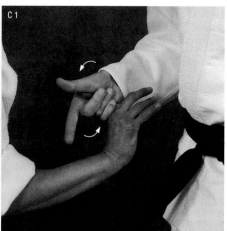

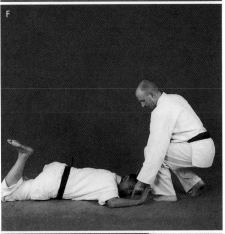

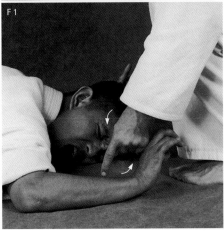

B. Finger Lock (pinky fulcrum)

Attacker applies a bear-hug, with their R hand overlapping their L hand. Your arms are pinned (A). Form a fist with your R hand and place it against the back of attacker's R hand (if their L hand is on top, use your L fist). Drive or rake your R thumb knuckles, or finger knuckles, into sensitive nerves between the metacarpal bones—typically N-UE-19a, M-UE-24, M-UE-50, or TW-3. Use your L hand to push the R hand (B1). As the grip loosens, peel back one or more fingers. This example shows the index finger. Wrap the R index finger with your L hand, placing your smallest finger on the base joint. Pull with your two smallest fingers, while pushing the fingertip with your palm (C, C1). Drive attacker's fingertip toward their forearm, with their palm facing down. This creates pain and forces them to drop (D). If their palm doesn't face down, they can't drop. As soon as attacker drops, turn toward them and step away, as you continue locking their finger, forcing them to their belly (E–F). Force is applied using a tight circular motion.

Important Points

In order to execute this technique, your lower arms must be free to move (A). If they are not, try to shift the bear-hug toward your elbows by lifting your arms, or by twisting and dropping your body. When you can reach attacker's hands, then proceed. There are many pressure points on the hand that can be pressed or pinched to break an attacker's grip. Further information can be found in the author's books, *Essential Anatomy for Healing and Martial Arts*, and *Hapkido: Traditions, Philosophy, Technique*.

N-UE-19a

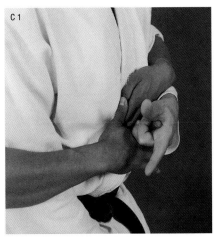

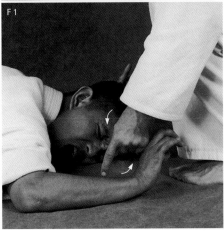

A

B

C

C. Finger Lock (index fulcrum)

From a relaxed stance (A), step forward with your R foot. Grip one or more fingers of opponent's R hand, placing your extended index finger on their base joints (B). Lock the fingers by rotating your hand, as you lever the fingertips toward the thumb-side of the back of their hand (C). Unbalance opponent to their right rear-corner and force a fall by pulling their hand downward and behind them (D). If their palm faces down, they will drop. If you turn their palm up, they will be forced to tiptoe (see next technique).

Important Points

The specific finger(s) you grip depends upon circumstances and opportunity. One-finger or two-finger holds work best, since an opponent has less strength to resist, although four-finger holds can also be effective. You can also grip four fingers initially, then let two fingers slip free as you apply circular leverage. Generally, try to grip the two smallest fingers, since they are the weakest. Force is applied using a tight circular motion.

D

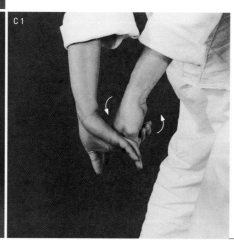

C 1

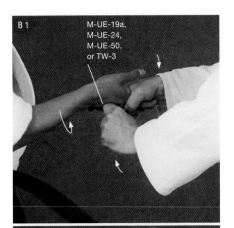

M-UE-19a,
M-UE-24,
M-UE-50,
or TW-3

D. Finger Lock (index fulcrum)

From a false handshake (A), grip tightly and twist attacker's palm up, as you drive your index-finger knuckle into a pressure point on the back of the hand (B). As attacker's grip loosens, slip your hand out and grip the two smallest fingers, pressing your index finger against the back of the base joints. Rotate your hand as you leverage their fingertips toward their forearm. This will force attacker to tiptoe (C). You can use this hold to restrain them while standing, escort them to another location, or pin them by using the following transition.

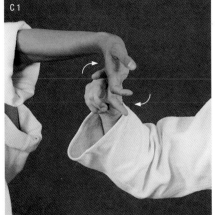

Transition to a Pin

Maintain the finger lock as you turn attacker's hand so their fingers point toward their shoulder, with their palm facing up. Attacker will turn away to relieve pain (D). Maintain the finger lock as you pull attacker's hand backward and down (E), forcing a Back Fall (F). This also locks the shoulder. The takedown leads directly to a pin. Pin attacker's palm against the ground as you continue levering their fingers toward their forearm. Their elbow is fully bent and pointing up, with their hand pinned near their shoulder. Kneel on their shoulder if needed (G).

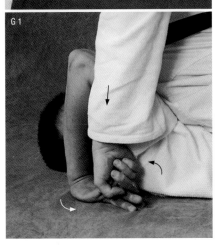

E. Twin Thumb Lock

Attacker steps inward to apply a choke, with their arms extended. As their hands approach your throat (A), step back with your L foot, reach over their hands, and grip both thumbs (B). Step back with your R foot, twist their hands outward, and bend both thumbs back to lock the joints (C). Wrap the thumbs with your smallest fingers on the base joints. Pull with the two smallest fingers, as you push with your palm. Continue to step backward as you force them to fall prone. Continue to lock the thumbs, pinning their elbows (D).

Important Points

Stepping back as you grip the thumbs gives you time to secure your grips, by delaying attacker's entry. Plant your thumbs (tip down) on the inner thumbs. This keeps attacker from pressing their thumbs into your throat. Lever their thumbs toward the *edge* of their forearms, using a tight circular motion. Modulate pressure using a pulsing, jerky motion to keep them from twisting their hand or using strength to counter. Use your upper-body weight to strengthen the pin if needed.

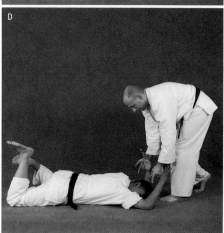

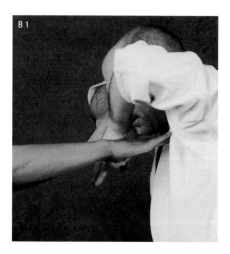

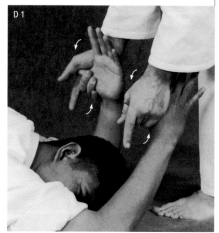

F. Turning Bent-Thumb Lock

Attacker grabs your belt, with their palm facing up (A). Hit or press PC-6 (above the wrist) using an Index Finger Fist (A1). As attacker's grip loosens, use your L thumb to twist their bent-thumb outward and down, as your L index finger pulls their base joint inward and up. At the same time, grip their wrist with your R hand (overhand grip) and twist their arm outward, to assist the thumb lock (B). The wrist and thumb will lock outward. Continue locking the joints, as you step across with your R foot and plant it outside attacker's R foot, blocking their leg (C) and forcing a fall (D). This hold can also force a fall without blocking the leg.

Index Finger Fist

Important Points

The pain of the thumb lock will usually release attacker's grip on your belt. If not, or if their hand is trapped, your body-pivot becomes more important, since it helps lock the wrist, unbalances your attacker, and forces them to the ground. If an attacker grips tightly, making it difficult to grip their thumb, use the next technique to loosen it, then apply this hold.

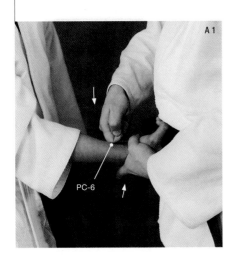

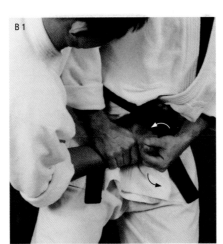

G. Boxing Thumb Lock

A standing attacker grabs your lapel while you are seated (A). Reach across with your L hand and lock their L thumb: use the heel of your palm to jam the tip of their bent-thumb toward its base joint, as you squeeze with your fingers to assist (B). As attacker releases your lapel, continue locking their thumb and turn their hand outward (B2). This motion will usually force attacker to fall sideways or drop to their knees. If you require greater strength or leverage, continue lock the thumb as you grasp four fingers with your R hand (overhand grip). Squeeze attacker's fingers together, clashing the joints, as you twist their hand outward (C). This locks the wrist and fingers, forcing a fall toward their left side (D).

Important Points

The thumb lock is quite strong and can be used to lead an opponent in many different directions. The second part of this technique is essentially a transition to an Outward Wrist Lock (covered in *Wrist Locks* chapter), which uses a four-finger hold to strengthen the lock.

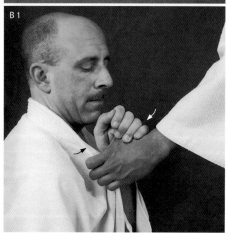

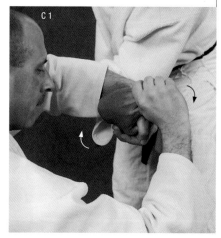

H. Cross-Arm Finger Locks

This is an attacking technique. From a relaxed stance (A), step quickly forward with your R foot. Grab all four fingers on both hands (B) and squeeze the fingers together, clashing the joints. Twist both hands counterclockwise and lock opponent's finger joints by levering their fingertips toward the backs of their hands. Cross their arms by passing their R hand under their L arm. Step under the arms with your L foot (C) and pivot 180° (D). Continue twisting the fingers: the L wrist locks inward, and the R wrist locks outward (D1). Break the joints or force a fall. A skilled opponent will initiate a high breakfall to save their joints and relieve pressure (E).

Important Points

This is a very effective hold, which will lock the fingers and wrists of both hands. Stepping under opponent's arms and pivoting, increases leverage on their fingers, wrist, and arm. Stepping also displaces your body to make counterstrikes difficult, which is particularly useful against multiple attackers. During step D, the R wrist locks outward, similar to an Outward Wrist Lock; and the L wrist locks inward, similar to an Elevated Wrist Lock. Both holds were shown in the *Wrist Locks* chapter.

Leg locks are holds in which force is primarily applied to the joints, tendons, ligaments, and bones of the leg, ankle, or foot. Sometimes considerable stress is also transferred to other anatomical structures, such as the hip and spine, depending upon the specific hold. While some leg locks can be used to force a takedown, most are pinning techniques that are commonly employed to restrain or immobilize an attacker, after they have been thrown using other techniques. This chapter outlines twelve basic leg locks commonly used in

LEG LOCKS

Hapkido and other martial arts. The first several pages will describe basic principles, followed by a quick overview of the twelve holds, to help you to understand their fundamental qualities and inherent relationships to each other. Subsequent pages then show each hold, in detail, being executed in a typical self-defense situation, as a finishing hold after a throw. Many other throwing techniques that incorporate leg locks, such as throws used against kicks, can be found in the author's companion book, "The Art of Throwing."

LEG LOCKS

When applying leg locks, the primary targets are the knee, ankle, Achilles tendon, back of the calf, toes, or hip joints. Generally, most leg locks involve leveraging or twisting attacks to joints. Try to use pressure points or nerves to assist your techniques. The most important points are: SP-6 and LV-6 on the inner shin; ST-34, ST-35, SP-10, SP-9, and N-LE-7 at the front corners of the knee; BL-54 at the back of the knee; BL-56 and BL-57 on the calf; BL-51 on the back of the thigh; and the nerves within the Achilles tendon. Since the leg is very powerful, pressing nerves is essential, to keep from being tossed about as you attempt to secure a hold. The leg locks described below and shown on the following pages are among those most commonly used. Many other variations and techniques exist.

1–3 Leg Bars

A leg bar is a type of leg lock in which the leg is fully extended, with the knee locked. Similar to an arm bar, force is applied at two points, in opposite directions—at the ankle and just above the kneecap. Locking the ankle and/or pressing above the kneecap at ST-34 or SP-10, will increase efficiency by creating pain and reducing leg strength.

1. Buttock Leg Bar

This hold is primarily used to counter a hold from behind. Lock the opponent's knee and force a fall backward, by lifting the ankle with both hands as you sink your buttock down and backward into the knee. Fall onto the knee if you wish to break it. Otherwise, step forward and away, or make a transition to a *Scissor Leg Bar* (next technique).

2. Scissor Leg Bar

This hold is primarily used to restrain an attacker after a takedown or throw. Plant the back of your knee above the opponent's knee; place the front of your thigh on the Achilles tendon. Scissor your legs to lock the knee. Use your hand or forearm to keep the foot extended, by pressing against the toes or instep. This reduces leg strength and keeps an opponent from kicking-out of the hold.

3. Two-Hand Leg Bar

Trap the opponent's ankle between your head and shoulder. At the same time, lock the opponent's knee and pull it toward you by driving both of your wrists into SP-10 and ST-34 (above the kneecap). If you are having difficulty maintaining control (not unlikely), sink your knee into the groin to assist the hold. Attacking nerves is crucial or you may not be able to keep an opponent from bending their leg and kicking-out of the hold.

4. Twisting Leg Lock + Knee Pin

This hold is primarily used to restrain an attacker after a throw. Twist the attacker's foot with both hands, as you drive your Knife Foot into the other knee at SP-10. As long as you keep the leg fully twisted, your opponent will not be able to kick-out of the hold. From here, you can also shift to holds 9–12.

5–6 Achilles Ankle Locks

In these holds, you will trap the extended foot in your armpit, wrap the ankle tightly, and leverage your wrist (radius bone) upward into the Achilles tendon. This is very painful, as along as the foot remains extended. These holds are commonly used to control the leg after a throw, and to force an opponent to roll over onto their belly. From here, these holds usually transition into *Crab Locks* (holds 7–8) or *Bent-Leg Locks* (holds 9–12).

7–8 Crab Locks

Hold one or both legs using an *Achilles Ankle Lock* (previous techniques). Sit backward, forcing the opponent's leg muscles, hip joint, and spine to travel beyond normal limits. Dropping forcefully is devastating, and rarely justified. When training, exercise extreme caution to prevent fracturing spinal vertebrae.

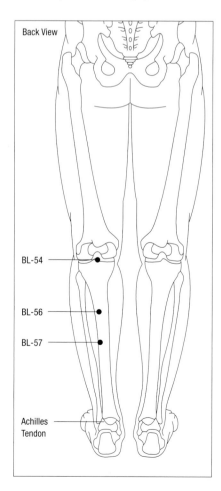

9–11 Bent-Leg Locks

Pin an opponent's bent-leg behind them, forcing their foot toward their buttock. Pain is created either by trapping your ankle in their inner knee (pain or joint separation), by pressing nerves at the calf or ankle, or by forcing the knee to bend beyond its normal limit. Always keep the opponent's foot fully extended, since this reduces their leg strength. If you allow them to bend their foot, they can usually kick-out of the hold.

9. Bent-Leg Lock (knee-body lever)
Lean forward. Force the knee to close tightly around the protruding bone of your ankle.

10. Bent-Leg Lock (wrist-body lever)
Push the instep down with your shoulder. Pull the calf to your chest with your wrist at BL-57.

11. Bent-Leg Lock (inner-thigh lever)
Push the instep down with your inner thigh. Apply a choke or pull the head back.

12. Cross Leg Pin

Trap one leg inside the other, and pull one instep backward, using both hands. You can trap the opponent's ankle in their inner knee, or against the back of their calf, or against the back of their Achilles tendon. Regardless of the method used, keep the opponent's foot extended and their knees fully bent, to keep them from kicking-out of the hold. Plant your buttocks on the spine and lean back slowly. Be sure to pull the instep, not the ankle.

1. Buttock Leg Bar

2. Scissor Leg Bar

3. Two-Hand Leg Bar

4. Twisting Leg Lock + Knee Pin

5. Achilles Ankle Lock

6. Twin Achilles Ankle Lock

7. Single-Leg Crab Lock

8. Twin-Leg Crab Lock

9. Bent-Leg Lock (knee-body lever)

10. Bent-Leg Lock (wrist-body lever)

11. Bent-Leg Lock (inner-thigh lever)

12. Cross-Leg Pin

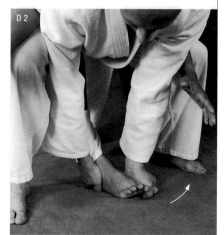

1. Buttock Leg Bar

Attacker pins your arms, with one foot forward (A). Thrust the back of your upper skull into the nose or face (B). Thrust your Live-Hands forward and buttocks backward, to break the hold and unbalance attacker backward (C). Grip attacker's ankle with both hands (D). Two possible grips are shown (D1, D2). Pull up, locking the knee on your buttock. Force a Back Fall (E). You can also sit back on the knee to break it. As attacker falls, step forward and away, or shift to the next technique (pin).

Important Points

In D1, both hands lift the ankle. This provides the strongest lift, but requires grip changes after throwing, in order to secure the leg. Any time you shift grips, you provide opportunity for counters. In D2, your outside-hand grips the heel, your inside-hand grips the inner edge of the foot, near the big toe. Grip changes are not required when shifting to leg locks (see technique 2 and 4). This permits constant control of the attacker's foot and leg. Some martial arts classify this technique as a hold, others classify it as a throw.

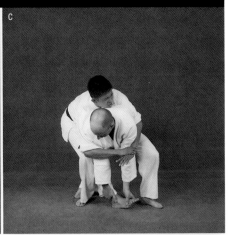

2. Scissor Leg Bar

This pin is used to restrain an attacker after a throw. Attacker pins your arms, with one foot forward (A). Lift your Live-Hands, step back with your R foot. Plant your thigh above their knee (B). Grab the ankle and foot with both hands (C). Lift up to lock the knee, forcing a Back Fall (D). Continue to lock the knee with the back of your knee. Trap the foot on your thigh, and twist your hips (E). Push the toes or instep back, keeping the foot extended. This keeps attacker from kicking-out of the hold.

Important Points

Be cautious during practice, since the knee can be hyperextended or broken quite easily. Knee locks do not produce pain as quickly as arm bars; thus, by the time pain registers, damage has usually already occurred. When controlling and pinning the leg (E), try to keep the foot fully extended, since this significantly reduces attacker's leg strength. If the foot is not extended, it will be very difficult for you to maintain control. If attacker turns onto their side to unlock their leg, they can counter by unbalancing you.

3. Two-Hand Leg Bar

This pinning technique is typically used to restrain an opponent after a throw or take-down. Attacker applies a Side Naked Choke. Relieve pressure by pulling their arm down with your R hand (A). Plant your L palm under their chin and your R hand behind their knee (B). Lift the underside of their chin backward with your L palm, as you scoop their knee forward, gouging BL-54 or KI-10. Unbalance attacker backward and throw them to their rear (C–D). Brace their ankle on your shoulder and lock their knee by joining your hands and driving your wrist or thumb-knuckle into SP-10. Sink your lower leg into their groin (E).

Important Points

When pushing the head back, you can also gouge your fingertips into the eyes, cheek, or throat; or reach behind the neck to the far shoulder and pull ST-11. When applying the leg lock, attacker's ankle is trapped between your neck and hunched shoulder (E). Accurate targeting of SP-10 is essential or you may not be able to control the leg, since it possesses very powerful muscles.

Press SP-10

A

B

C

4. Twisting Leg Lock + Knee Pin

This hold is used to restrain an attacker after a throw. Execute steps A–D as described in technique 1, using grip D2. As attacker falls, twist their foot outward with both hands. Pivot 180° on your R foot and deliver a L Side Kick to the head (E). Twist attacker's foot counterclockwise with both hands (F1), as you pin their knee by pressing your Knife Foot into SP-10 (F). If you can keep attacker's leg fully twisted, they cannot kick-out of the hold. If you lose control, stomp the groin.

Important Points

If you throw using grip D1 (see technique 1), you will need to shift your L hand up toward the toes, as attacker falls. You can also pin the knee with your sole or heel. The sole is very stable, but does not target nerves as effectively as the Knife Foot, since it is a broad, flat surface. The heel targets nerves fairly well, but can easily slip off the leg if you are not accurate when planting it, or the knee shifts. In contrast, the Knife Foot offers a longer surface with greater margin for error.

D

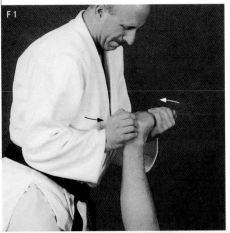

F 1

Knife Foot

E

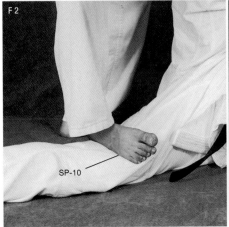

F 2

SP-10

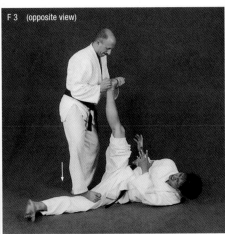

F 3   (opposite view)

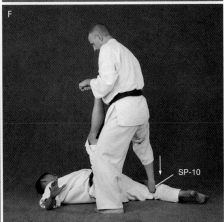

F

SP-10

B

A

C

D

5. Achilles Ankle Lock

This pinning technique is used to restrain an opponent after a throw. As attacker delivers a lead straight punch, charge to their right side and parry inward with your L hand (A–B). Lower your body, drop your R knee toward the ground, and plant your R wrist on the inner knee at SP-9 or SP-10. Grip the heel with your L hand (C). Push the knee outward as you scoop the heel inward, forcing a fall (D). Lift the ankle to your R armpit. Wrap it tightly, keeping the foot extended. Join your hands and lock the ankle by levering your R radius bone upward into the Achilles tendon (E). Stand up to increase pain (F).

Important Points

If attacker attempts to kick you with their free leg, pivot your body and lever your wrist slightly sideways to turn them away (F). This hold can also be applied by standing between the legs, instead of on the outside. However, this is more risky, since you can be easily kicked. The Achilles Ankle Hold is often used to shift to a Single-Leg Crab Lock (technique 7) or a Bent-Leg Lock (technique 9).

Keep the Foot Extended

Always keep your opponent's foot fully extended, throughout this technique. This reduces the strength of their leg muscles and increases the level of pain at the Achilles tendon. If your opponent can manage to fully bend their foot, their tolerance to pain will increase substantially, and they will possess greater strength in their legs to resist or kick-out of the hold. The ankle lock is very painful and effective, as along as the foot remains fully extended and the nerve is targeted.

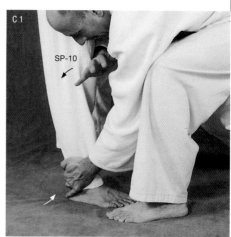

C 1

SP-10

E

F (opposite view)

F 1

6. Twin Achilles Ankle Lock

This pinning technique is used to restrain an opponent after a takedown or throw. As attacker pushes with both hands, step back with either foot, absorb the push, and bring both hands up between attacker's arms (A). As they continue pushing, deflect both arms outward with the blades of your hands (B). Lower your upper body and allow attacker's momentum to carry them into you. Drive your shoulder into their torso to unbalance them. Grip the backs of both knees and lift to throw (C–D). As attacker falls, wrap both ankles in your armpits, keeping the feet extended (E). Lock both ankles by levering your radius bones upward into the Achilles tendon (F).

Important Points

This hold is the same as the previous hold, except both ankles are locked simultaneously. The lock is very painful as long as attacker's foot remains fully extended. If they can bend their foot, their tolerance to pain is much greater and they will possess more leg strength to resist. This hold often leads to a Twin-Leg Crab Lock (technique 8).

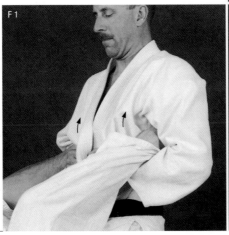

C

B

A

D

7. Single-Leg Crab Lock

This pinning technique is used to restrain an opponent after a takedown or throw. Execute steps A–E as described in technique 5. Stand up and pivot, as you lever your radius bone upward, then laterally into the Achilles tendon (F). This forces attacker to turn onto their belly. Continue to lift and twist their ankle, as you plant your R foot between their legs (G). Step over their hips with your L foot. Sit on the spine and lean backward, forcing the leg muscles, ankle, and spine to travel beyond their normal limits (H). Exercise extreme caution. Dropping forcefully will fracture spinal vertebrae.

Important Points

When locking the ankle (E), you can join your hands or grip your lapel for support, or use one hand only. Begin locking the ankle and *turning* attacker as soon as they land (F), to prevent being kicked by their free leg. As you step, press your L knee and lower leg sideways, then down into the lower spine (G). This assists the turnover and helps restrain attacker's movement as you step over them.

Keep the Foot Extended

Keep your opponent's foot fully extended throughout this technique. This reduces the strength of opponent's leg muscles and increases the level of pain at the Achilles tendon. If your opponent can manage to fully bend their foot, their tolerance to pain will increase substantially, and they will possess greater strength in their legs to resist or kick-out of the hold. The ankle lock is very painful and effective, as along as the foot remains fully extended.

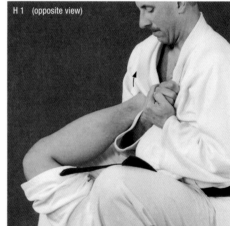

H 1 (opposite view)

E

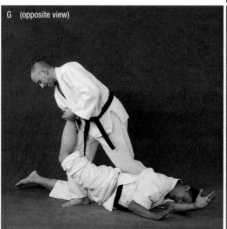

F (opposite view)

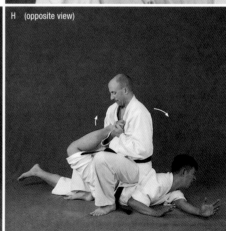

G (opposite view)

H (opposite view)

8. Twin-Leg Crab Lock

This pinning technique is used to restrain an opponent after a takedown or throw. Execute steps A–D as described in technique 6.

As attacker falls, wrap both ankles in your armpits, keeping the feet extended (E). Lock both ankles by levering your radius bones upward into the Achilles tendon (F), applying a Twin Achilles Ankle Lock (same as technique 6). Pivot your body as you lever your radius bones upward, then laterally into the Achilles tendons. This forces attacker to turn onto their belly. Continue to lift and twist the ankles, as you step over their body with one leg. Lean back, forcing the leg muscles, ankle, and spine to travel beyond their normal limits (G). Exercise extreme caution or you may fracture spinal vertebrae.

Important Points

This hold is the same as the previous hold, except both ankles are locked simultaneously. Be sure to keep both feet fully extended, with the ankles locked, to prevent counters. Please reference the notes given for the previous technique, since they also pertain to this hold.

C

B

A

D

9. Bent-Leg Lock (knee-body lever)

This pinning technique is used to restrain an opponent after a takedown or throw. Execute steps A–D as described in technique 5. Stand up and pivot, as you lever your radius bone upward, then laterally into the Achilles tendon (E). This forces attacker to turn onto their belly. Continue to lift and twist their ankle, as you plant your R foot between their legs (F). Step over their hips with your L foot and pivot (G). Let the ankle to slip from your armpit. Using both hands, grip the ankle and pull back on the toes. Keep the foot extended or you will lose control. Plant your R shin or ankle across the back of attacker's knee, and place their instep on your belly or chest (H). Lean forward as you push your knee backward (I). This is painful and will dislocate the knee if you go too far.

Important Points

The entry is similar to technique 7, except you will pivot another 180° as you step over. Leaning forward forces attacker's knee to close tightly around the protruding bone of your ankle. To increase pain, *lever your knee backward* as you lean forward.

Keep the Foot Extended

Always keep your opponent's foot fully extended, throughout this technique. This reduces the strength of their leg muscles and increases the level of pain at the Achilles tendon. If your opponent can manage to fully bend their foot, their tolerance to pain will increase substantially, and they will possess greater strength in their legs to resist or kick-out of the hold. This hold is very effective, as along as the foot remains fully extended, particularly during your entry.

E (opposite view)

I (opposite view)

F (opposite view)

G (opposite view)

H (opposite view)

10. Bent-Leg Lock (wrist-body lever)

This pinning technique is used to restrain an opponent after a throw. A seated defense is shown as an example; however, many other entries are possible. While you are seated, attacker executes a Front Kick (A). Block with your forearms crossed and grab their ankle (R hand over L, for R kick). Twist their foot as you pull it toward you, trapping it between your inner elbow and shoulder (B). Plant one or both wrists on their calf at BL-57 and press down, forcing a Front Fall (C). Pin by pressing your wrist into BL-56, BL-57, or the Achilles tendon, as you push attacker's instep downward with your shoulder (D). Their knee is fully bent and their foot is fully extended.

Important Points

Two alternate methods of attacking the nerves on the calf are shown in D1 and D2. In either method, use the bony part of your wrist to attack nerves on the calf, pull the lower leg tight to your body, and keep attacker's foot fully extended throughout the technique. This reduces leg strength and increases the level of pain at the Achilles tendon. If an opponent can manage to bend their foot, their tolerance to pain will increase substantially, and they will possess greater leg strength to resist or kick-out of the hold. If your hands are reversed during the initial block (L hand over R, for R kick), you must apply technique 12 instead.

A

B

C

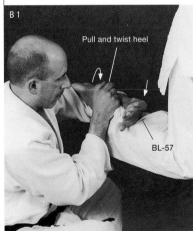

B 1

Pull and twist heel

BL-57

D 1

D 2

D

Outer Forearm

11. Bent-Leg Lock (inner-thigh lever)

This pin is used to restrain an opponent after a throw. Charge inward as you duck beneath a Spin Kick or Hook Kick, raising your R hand to provide a block if needed (A). Grip attacker's ankle with your L hand, as you thrust your R outer wrist or forearm into the side or back of their knee (B). Pull the ankle upward to your L armpit (trap), as you drive their knee downward, forcing a Front Fall (C). Bend attackers leg behind them, as you step forward and straddle them. Release your arm-hold on the ankle, as you transfer pressure to their instep by pressing it downward with your inner thigh. Lean forward and lower your hips, pinning their foot against their buttock. Apply a Rear Naked Choke (D) with your R arm, or pull the head back with your hands to lock the neck.

Important Points
As you straddle attacker, maintain constant pressure on the lower leg as you transfer it from your arm to your thigh. Keep their foot extended by pressing your thigh against the toes or instep, not the ankle. Sink your hips slowly and gently to avoid breaking the ankle.

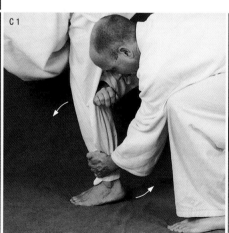

Pin Leg

A

B

C

12. Cross-Leg Pin

This pinning technique is used to restrain an opponent after a throw. A seated defense is shown as an example; however, many other entries are possible. While you are seated, attacker executes a Front Kick (A). Block with your forearms crossed and grab their ankle (L hand over R, for R kick). Twist their foot as you pull it toward you, trapping it between your inner elbow and shoulder (B). Press down and twist, forcing a Side Fall (C). Continue twisting the foot to turn them onto their belly (D). Keep the instep extended and twisted (D1), as you circle to your right. Place their R ankle on the back of their L knee and grip their L instep, as you straddle and sit on their lower spine (E). Pull the instep of the L foot backward with both hands, trapping the right leg inside the left (F).

Important Points

As you straddle attacker (D–E), they will often kick or bring the L foot toward you, making it easy to grab. As you pull the instep and lean backward (F), the trapped R ankle presses nerves on the L leg, causing extreme pain and eventually forcing the knee to dislocate.

D

E

B 1

Pull and twist heel

Press BL-57

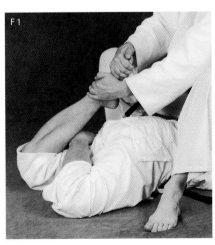

D 1   (opposite view)

F 1

F

Chokes and head locks are specific types of holds that are applied to the neck and head. "Chokes holds" typically involve strangulation techniques designed to impede or stop the flow of blood or air to the brain, whereas "head locks" are joint lock techniques used to apply stress to the cervical spine. Both types of holds are potentially very dangerous and can easily produce life-threatening injuries. For this reason, these techniques should only be learned and practiced under qualified instructors, who are also skilled in revival techniques. When

CHOKES + HEAD LOCKS

these techniques are properly and skillfully applied in appropriate situations, they provide one of the most powerful and effective methods for controlling an opponent, without causing serious or permanent injuries. As opponents become larger and more powerful, any martial technique tends to lose its effectiveness, although chokes remain useful longer than most other skills. The following pages will provide an overview of basic principles, followed by a description of 32 chokes and head locks commonly used in the martial arts.

BASIC CONCEPTS

Chokes and head locks are specific types of holds applied to the neck and head. They are typically used to control or restrain a person, and work in one or more of three ways: by reducing the flow of blood or air to the brain via strangulation, by applying painful pressure to nerves and pressure points, or by twisting the head to stress the cervical spine.

Chokes

Choke holds are commonly applied to the neck, using your hands, arms, legs, or feet. The surfaces of your body used to apply chokes will vary by technique, and are mostly the same as surfaces used for striking (see *Attack Points* at right). Chokes can be used to render an opponent unconscious, assist throws, or weaken an attacker during grappling. There are three types of chokes:

• Vascular Chokes (restrict blood flow)
• Windpipe Chokes (restrict air flow)
• Nerve Chokes (control movement and pain)

Vascular Chokes

Vascular chokes reduce or eliminate the flow of blood to the brain, resulting in progressive disorientation, loss of consciousness, or death. This usually involves clamping holds to the carotid artery, jugular vein, and vagus nerve, all in close proximity on the side of the neck. By compressing blood vessels, blood flow is decreased and pressure increases. The vagus nerve, which normally acts to slow the heart rate in response to supply demands, further reduces blood flow, compounding the effect. When a vascular choke is properly applied, an opponent can pass out in 10 to 15 seconds. While this person may regain consciousness naturally, many chokes lead to a loss of breathing and heart functions, in which case it is vital to revive the person, or brain damage and death will quickly occur. When using vascular chokes, accuracy is essential if the choke is to be effective. Primary targets are ST-9 and ST-10 (where a pulse is felt). Chokes at SI-17 are also possible, but require greater accuracy. Vascular chokes are not usually painful unless nerves are also being pressed.

Windpipe Chokes

Windpipe chokes reduce or eliminate the flow of air to the brain, resulting in progressive disorientation, loss of consciousness, or death. Chokes to the windpipe are very dangerous and should only be used in life threatening situations. A collapsed trachea is likely, which requires immediate expert medical attention to prevent death. Windpipe chokes do not require the precise accuracy of vascular chokes to be effective. They are easier to learn and often applied accidentally by novices attempting to learn vascular chokes. Generally, vascular chokes are preferred for most situations, since they are safer.

Nerve Chokes

Nerve chokes attack nerves or pressure points in order to control an opponent's movements by producing pain or damaging motor functions. Many of these sensitive points will work even on powerful opponents. Targets include LI-18, SI-16, TW-17, CO-22, ST-9, ST-10, and the spinal nerves at the back of the neck. Properly directed, nerve chokes can produce intense pain, forcing a submission or causing a loss of consciousness. Nerve chokes are often combined with vascular chokes.

Head Locks

Head locks are typically characterized by twisting the head to stress the cervical spine and its nerves. Head-twisting holds limit mobility by damaging the spine, or pinching spinal nerves where they pass through the vertebrae. Violent head-twisting is *extremely dangerous*, and should only be used in life threatening situations. A broken neck is likely and can cause permanent paralysis or death. In contrast, gentle head-twisting is safer, and a very efficient way to control body movement, particularly on the ground. Some head locks also incorporate choking techniques.

Practical Concerns

In terms of application, there are two forms of chokes: those that rely on clothing or the environment for support (lapel, wall, ground), and those that do not. It is important to evaluate a situation before applying a choke.

For example, a Lapel Choke is not used on an opponent clothed in a T-shirt (or shirtless), since this choke requires strong clothing to be effective. In this situation, you might use a Naked Choke or an Interlock Choke. Another example: if your opponent is backed against a wall, a Forearm Thrust Choke (using your arm to pin the neck against the wall) is far more efficient than attempting to wrap your entire arm around the head (Front Naked Choke).

Limitations of Chokes

It is important to understand the limitations of various chokes. Some individuals possess tremendous ability to resist all forms of chokes; others are easily restrained, even when your technique is bad. Only by sparring or engaging in competition can you become fluent with choke techniques. Work lightly and sensibly, under qualified supervision.

It is also important to realize that some chokes used in competition (e.g., Judo) were specifically modified for sport use. Rules often limit technique or encourage methods of application that would be inherently risky in self-defense. For example, when applying a Rear Naked Choke in Judo, your head is often placed to the side of an opponent's head, to secure a stronger hold and restrict head motion. In a real fight, this places your face within striking distance, allowing an opponent to poke your eyes or punch back to the face. This response is not legal in Judo competition, hence not a concern. If you were originally trained to choke in competitive martial arts, you may need to modify certain aspects of your technique—although basic principles remain the same.

Choke Transitions

Skillful opponents may negate your attempts to choke them. Switching between vascular, windpipe, and nerve chokes is often useful if an opponent protects one area. For example, if an opponent drops the chin to protect the windpipe, circle your hand around to the side of the neck and attack the carotid artery or great auricular nerve (LI-18). Strikes can also create the space needed to apply a choke.

Types of Chokes

Windpipe Choke (restricts air flow)

Vascular Choke (restricts blood flow)

Nerve Choke (controls movement, causes pain)

Major Targets

A. Windpipe (CO-23)
B. Base of Windpipe (CO-22)
C. Jugular Vein ····
D. Carotid Artery ---
E. LI-18 (4 nerves)
F. SI-16 (2 nerves, cervical a.)
G. SI-17 (carotid a., jugular v., 3 nerves)
H. ST-9 (branching of carotid a., thyroid a., jugular v., 3 nerves)
I. ST-10 (common carotid a., cut. cervical n., superior cardiac n.)
J. TW-17 (auricular n., jugular v.)
K. Spinal Nerves

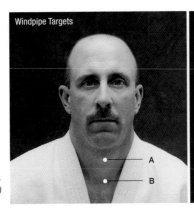

Windpipe Targets

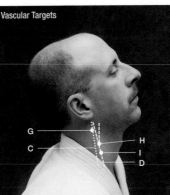

Vascular Targets

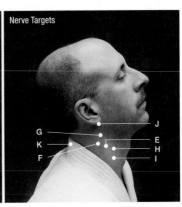

Nerve Targets

Attack Points

The following attack points are generally used to apply chokes. Many other possibilities exist.

A. Fingertips
B. Tip of Thumb
C. Finger Knuckles
D. Index Finger Knuckle
E. Pincer Hand
F. Tiger Mouth Hand
G. Knife Hand (edge of hand)
H. Wrist (protruding bones)
H. Forearm (edge of bone)
I. Lower Leg (edge of bone)
J. Foot (blade, heel, or toes)

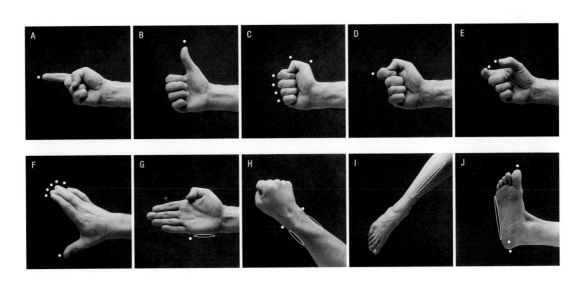

Basic Entries

When applying chokes in which you wrap the neck, there are two basic methods of entry:
A) Circle the neck, raking with your thumb knuckles; or
B) Execute a strike which places your attack point at the target to be choked.

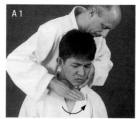   

Forced Entries

If an opponent drops the chin to protect the neck, press sensitive points to move their head.

C. TW-17 (behind ear)
D. ST-4 (jaw)
E. GB-1 or TW-23 (temple)
F. Eyes and ST-2 (cheek)

Wrist Action

Regardless of how a choke is applied, wrist movement is very important when pressing your attack points into the neck. Three methods of executing a Naked Choke are shown as a typical example. Although the method of clasping the hands varies, wrist action is the same. The first method (1A–1B) is widely used and may be the most difficult grip to break. The second and third methods (2A–2B; 3A–3B) sometimes permit deeper penetration and greater force. Generally, body position, individual anatomy, and personal preference will all influence grip choice. The subtle differences are best grasped by experimentation.

Ki-Flow and Grip

When gripping your fist in methods 2 and 3, place HT-8 (palm between 4th and 5th metacarpal bones) against SI-3 (back of the smallest base-knuckle) Biomechanically, this provides a strong, secure grip.

Aligning these acupoints is also thought to increase physical strength, since the natural flow of Ki is enhanced (HT meridian connects with the SI meridian) In method 2, your smallest fingers will overlap each other, also aligning HT-9 and SI-1.

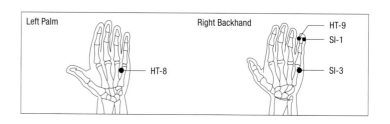

Eliminating Free-Play

The effectiveness of a choke is reduced when there is any free-play or movement in the hold. To restrict movement:

A. Use Lapel
B. Use Wall
C. Use Ground
D. Use Your Arm
E. Use Your Head
F. Use Opponent's Weight
G. Use Your Weight

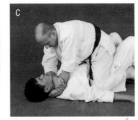

Body Positions

Most chokes can be executed from a variety of positions. Typical examples are shown opposite. Many other body relationships are possible.

A. Front Standing (upright)
B. Front Standing (bent over)
C. Side Standing
D. Rear Standing
E. Overhead Hanging
F. Rear Kneeling
G. Front Kneeling
H. Side Mount
I. Front Top-Mount
   (supine attacker)
J. Rear Top-Mount
   (prone attacker)
K. Front Reclining
L. Rear Reclining

CHOKE HOLDS

1. Front Naked Choke

Press your opponent's head downward (A), as you tightly wrap your arm around the neck, placing the bony part of your wrist or forearm against the throat. Join your hands as shown previously, using *wrist action* to apply (B, C). Lifting up and leaning back will place extreme stress on the cervical spine. This choke is a useful counter against a low charge or throws in which an opponent tries to scoop your legs from the front.

2. Rear Naked Choke

This is a very strong, practical choke. Tightly wrap your arm around the neck, placing the bony part of your wrist, forearm, or thumb-knuckles against the desired target. When standing, quickly unbalance an opponent to their rear by using a hip butt or palm strike (A) to the lower spine. This prevents counterthrows or escapes. Join your hands and use *wrist action* to apply (B, C). Opponent's *hanging body* will increase pressure.

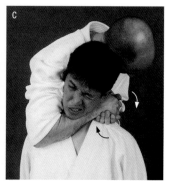

3. Front Lapel Choke

This choke requires strong clothing, since it uses an opponent's collar for support. Pull the lapel out and down with one hand; grip the collar at the side of the neck with the other hand (A). Rotate your fist, extending your wrist bone into the target. Pull the opposite lapel across the neck to create a *noose-like* effect (B). The choke is made stronger by using a wall (C) or the ground for support, to keep the neck from moving away.

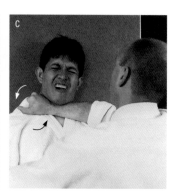

4. Rear Lapel Choke

This is similar to the previous choke, except it is applied from the rear. Reach around as far as possible and grip the collar at the far side (A). Extend the wrist into the throat as you pull the opposite lapel down and across the neck (B, C). The choke is stronger when using an opponent's hanging weight to increase pressure. When kneeling, stand up as you apply pressure. When standing, unbalance an opponent backward.

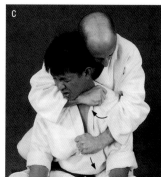

5. Front Double Lapel Choke

This is similar to a *Front Lapel Choke*, except you will use both hands. With your arms crossed, grip high on both sides of the collar. Apply pressure with both wrists. When choking from a straddle position, lean forward and press your elbows toward the ground (A–B). When standing, pull an opponent close and spread your elbows (C). Be cautious when using this choke, since it leaves you open to strikes (your hands are occupied; opponent's are free).

Double Lapel Grip Variations

There are three methods of gripping. In method 1, both hands grip with the thumbs *outside.* Rotate your wrists and spread the elbows to apply. In method 2, both hands grip with the thumbs *inside.* Use *wrist action* and spread your elbows to apply. In method 3 (not shown), the top hand grips with the thumb inside, the lower hand with the thumb outside. In the photos, the choker's head is dropped for a better view (don't do this).

6. Rear Double Lapel Choke

This is like a *Rear Lapel Choke,* except you will use both hands. With your arms crossed, grip high on both sides of the collar (A). Apply pressure by using *wrist action* and spreading your elbows (B, C). Since both arms cross under the chin, this hold also locks the neck backward (immobilizing the head), as you press to both sides of the throat at the carotid artery (ST-9, ST-10). This choke is very strong if your grips are properly placed.

7. Rear Cross Choke

This is basically a *Rear Lapel Choke,* except you will use your other forearm to apply additional pressure to the opposite side of the neck, often to nerves (A–C). This eliminates free-play and neck motion, which often reduces the efficiency of lapel chokes. The other wrist presses the carotid artery or windpipe. This choke can also be used to counter a throw when the opponent's body is placed in front of you (e.g., a hip throw).

A

B

C

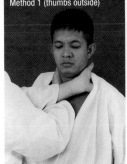
Method 1 (thumbs outside)

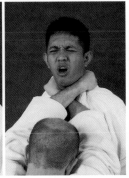

Method 2 (thumbs inside)

A

B

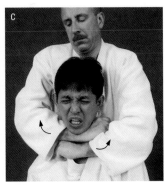
C

A

B

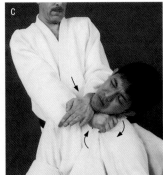
C

8. Half-Nelson Choke

This is similar to the previous *Rear Cross Choke,* except you will trap one arm by reaching under it and lifting, as you wrap your hand behind the head, turning your palm outward (A–B). Drive your hand around to the side of the neck, pressing with your Knife Hand as you choke with the other hand (C). This choke is useful if an opponent reaches back to attack your face during other chokes. When standing or kneeling, unbalance an opponent rearward and hang them from the choke (C).

Half-Nelson Variations
Provided the opponent is hanging, you can choke with your wrist placed at either side of the neck (D, E). Grip placement is not critical, since a loose choke will become tight as you apply it. When executed on the ground (F), drive or kick your heels into the groin. Keep your eyes away from the fingers of the held arm. Generally, these are very secure chokes, and are very difficult to counter or escape once they have been applied.

9. Double Sleeve Choke

In this choke you will use both sleeves for support. Place your arms on both sides of the neck. Grip your inner sleeves with both hands, and extend both wrists (or forearms) into the targets. This choke can be applied from any position (front, rear, side, ground). When ground fighting, this choke is difficult to detect, since your arms do not provide the usual clues to an opponent (e.g., wrapping the neck, gripping the collar, clasping your hands).

10. Single Sleeve Choke

This is similar to the previous choke, except you will grip one sleeve only. This is not by choice, but usually because your opponent does not allow you to secure the second grip—or you may feel that your hold is strong enough and does not warrant further maneuvering. If possible, use the ground, wall, or your body weight to assist the hold. Many positions are possible, including top (A), bottom (B), and side (C).

 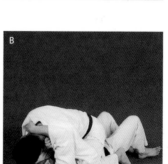 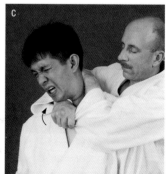

11. Arm Trap Choke

This is basically a *naked choke* applied from the side, with the opponent's arm trapped between your shoulder and their head. The choke can be entered by either wrapping or striking into the far side of the neck. Join your hands as shown previously, pressing your wrist or thumb-knuckles into the carotid artery or nerves (LI-18 is typical). Because the entry is very fast, it is often used to counter straight punches or pushes, by using a parry to deflect as you enter.

Ground Variations (D)

This choke is used to force a takedown, or is applied during ground-fighting. On the ground, the hold varies slightly: Wrap your arm further around the neck. Press your wrist and the edge of your tensed arm muscles into nerves or the carotid artery. To secure the hold, press down with your neck and head, place one leg against the side of the attacker's body (knee and ball of the foot planted), and brace outward with your other leg.

12. Rear Interlock Choke

This is another variation on a basic *Naked Choke.* It is mostly applied from the rear. Wrap the choking arm around the neck, locking your hand in the crook of your other elbow (A). Place your other hand behind the head and push forward with the edge of your Knife Hand or wrist, as you pull back with the choking forearm (B, C). Use pronounced *wrist action* with both arms. This is mostly a windpipe choke, so exercise caution.

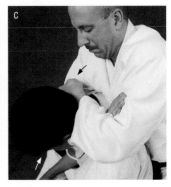

13. Front Interlock Choke

This is the same as the previous choke, except it is executed from the front. Two possibilities exist: *Front-over* (A) and *front-facing* (B or C). Front-over can be used from standing or ground postures. Front-facing is also used from standing or ground positions, however, you will be reversing the roles of your arms. The wrapping arm will be pressing nerves at the back of the neck. The other wrist or hand will press against the throat.

14. Arm Scissor Choke

This choke is applied from an opponent's side. Enter by placing your wrist at the base of the windpipe (A–B). Place your other forearm on the back of the neck, clasp the hands or interlock your fingers, and choke by extending both wrists (C). If needed, extend your arms to increase pressure. Secure the hold by dropping to one knee. This choke is often used as a transition from a *Front Naked Choke,* if an opponent turns outward to escape.

15. Arm Brace Choke

Wrap one hand behind the opponent's neck, with your fingertips at the far side, gouging nerves. Grab your wrist with the other hand, planting your forearm on the windpipe and carotid artery. Drive your elbow toward the back of the neck, as you pull with both hands (A, B). This choke is made more secure by using the ground (C) or wall for support. This choke's weakness is the open end of the hold, which permits escapes.

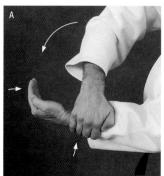 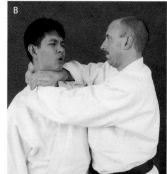 

16. Thrust Choke

Pull back on the lapels as you thrust your wrist into the front of the throat (A), or drive your smallest base-knuckle into ST-9 (B). This can be a gentle plant or a forceful strike. Use the wall or ground to eliminate movement whenever possible. You can also execute the choke with one hand, using the other hand to block or grab a strike (C). This choke is also used to initiate a throw, by trapping or reaping a leg as you drive an attacker backward.

 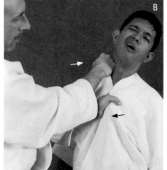 

17. Knuckle Choke

This choke is executed from the front, using a *Knuckle Fist* (A). Grip the lapels with both hands, placing your fingers inside the cloth. Take up slack and apply pressure by turning your fists outward, and driving the second set of knuckles into the front or sides of the neck. Whenever possible, use the wall, ground (B), or a neck wrap (C) to eliminate neck movement. This choke is very effective for targeting nerves or acupoints.

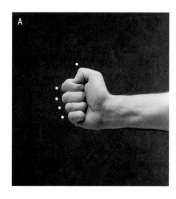 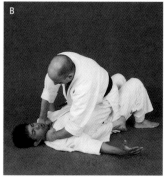 

18. Index Knuckle Choke

This is basically the same as the previous *Knuckle Choke*, except you will use an *Index Finger Fist* (A) to apply pressure. The extended knuckle will penetrate more deeply, and is used for pinpoint targeting to sensitive nerves and acupoints. The choke can be applied with two hands holding at the collar (B), or with one hand holding and pressing, as your other hand pulls the opposite lapel to tighten the choke (C).

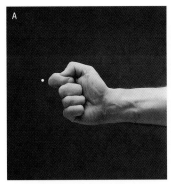

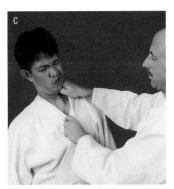

19. Thumb-Hand Choke

This choke is executed from the front or side, using a *Thumb Hand* (A) to apply pressure. The tip of the thumb is driven into any neck target, particularly nerves and acupoints. This choke can be applied with one or both hands by: gripping the collar for leverage (B), wrapping your fingers around the neck for support (C), or applying a straight thrust (no grips) and using the wall or ground to eliminate neck movement. Exercise caution.

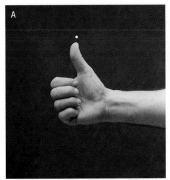
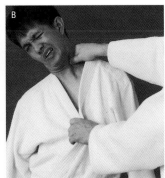
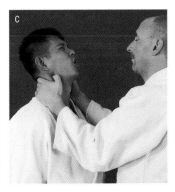

20. Spear-Hand Choke

This choke is executed from the front or rear, using a one, two, or three finger *Spear Hand* (A) to apply pressure. The finger may be straight or bent. The most common target is CO-22 at the base of the windpipe. You may trap the head by by pulling the lapel (B) or wrapping the neck (C). This choke is also used to apply throws, by pushing the throat as you pull the lower spine or trap a leg.

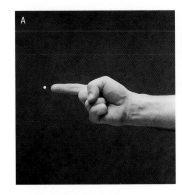
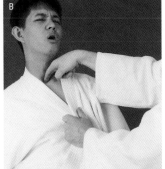
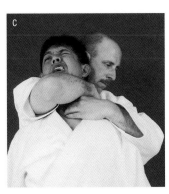

21. Tiger-Mouth Choke

Use a *Tiger Mouth Hand* to clamp the windpipe or press into both carotid arteries (A). Squeeze with all five fingertips, using clothing, holds, or the environment to eliminate movement.

22. Pincer-Hand Choke

Clamp with the thumb and index fingers (B). You can also assist by pressing with your lower knuckles. The photo shows an attack to CO-22 and ST-11.

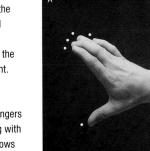

23. Knife-Foot Choke

This is often used to choke and pin an opponent immediately after you have thrown them. Press the blade of your foot into the throat or side of the neck, as you pull up on the arm (A–C). Shift your weight to the choke-leg as needed. You may enter the choke by planting the foot gently or striking forcefully. You may also apply an arm bar to the held-arm, to strengthen the technique (B). *Do not* step on the windpipe (life threatening).

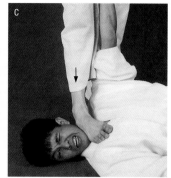

24. Knee Choke

Like the previous choke, this choke is also used to choke and pin, immediately after throwing an opponent. Sink your knee into the throat or side of the neck, as you pull up on the arm (A–C). Your planted knee remains on the ball of the foot, ready to rise or shift balance if an opponent counters. You can apply joint locks to strengthen the hold. If the situation justifies it, you may drop forcefully, thrusting your knee into the neck.

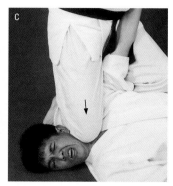

25. Leg Interlock Choke

Wrap one leg over an opponent's shoulder and around their neck, locking your foot in the back of your other knee (the other leg passes under their armpit). Fully bend both feet and drive your heel toward your buttock to tighten the choke (A). The opponent's arm must be trapped against their neck to eliminate space. You may also apply an arm bar (see A). If an opponent rolls, maintain your hold (B). There are many other variations.

26. Leg Scissor Choke

This hold is often used to counter chokes from the side, when you are reclining. Roll back and plant the back of one leg against the side of the neck (A). Reach around the head with your other leg and hook the ankles together (B). Drive both legs toward the ground. Press the knees together and extend the legs to choke (C). As you enter, grab the opponent's wrist with both hands to keep the from turning away. Arm bars are often possible.

CAUTION:
Head Locks can easily result in permanent disabilities or death. Practice only under qualified supervision.

27–29 Full Nelson Locks

This head lock is very dangerous and will break the neck if forcefully applied. Reach under both arms, slipping both hands behind the head. There are three methods of applying force to the spine: 1) Push forward with overlapped *palms* against the back of the opponent's head. 2) Push forward with *Knife Hands* projecting around the side of the neck, with wrists crossed. 3) *Compress* the cervical spine by pushing the head down.

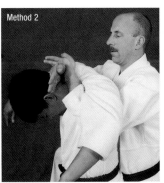

30. Twisting Neck Lock

If forcefully applied, this head lock will break the neck or dislocate the jaw (if the jaw is unclenched). However, if detected, the hold is easily countered by using strength. Push with the heel of your palm against the chin; pull with the other palm at the back of the head (C), or pull hair. When applied gently, it can be used to control the body, throw, or pin. Generally, the body will follow the head. Execute from ground (A) or standing (B) positions.

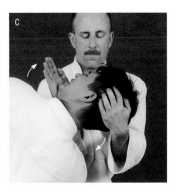

31. Scooping Neck Lock

Drive your thumb-knuckles into nerves at the side of the jaw (ST-4), and scoop upward using one or both hands to twist the head and neck (A–B). Attacking nerves is very important, otherwise an opponent can resist the hold (C). You can also press into the gums or teeth. Be *extremely careful* when twisting, or you may break the neck. This hold is often used to force your way into a *Front Naked Choke,* or to throw an opponent.

32. Smothering Neck Lock

Apply a *Rear Naked Choke* with one arm, to control head motion (A); try to clamp the windpipe or carotid artery. Place your other palm tightly over the opponent's mouth, pinching the nose closed with your thumb and index finger (B). Cup your hand to prevent being bitten. Tight holds totally block air intake. Even if air slips in, volume is greatly reduced, particularly if winded. "C" shows a ground choke using a hair-pull to assist (C).

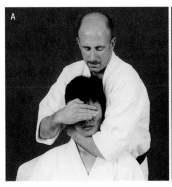
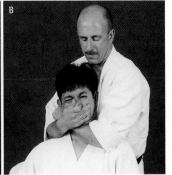

Nerve holds are used to control movement or generate pain by attacking sensitive nerves and pressure points anywhere on the body. Although these holds can be used by themselves to produce takedowns, initiate escapes, or immobilize opponents, they are usually a component part of other holding and throwing techniques. In this sense, nerve holds are often thought of as the useful additions that make other techniques more effective. The effectiveness of nerve holds largely depends on the skill of users, their knowledge of human

NERVE HOLDS

anatomy and Eastern medicine, their understanding of pressure point fighting principles, and their accuracy in targeting the right point at the right time. It is also important to realize that sensitivity to a specific hold varies widely by individual: the same point that causes intense pain in one person may leave another unaffected. This chapter outlines twelve basic nerve holds. Numerous other possibilities exist, many of which are shown in practical applications throughout this book, as an integral part of other techniques.

NERVE HOLDS

Nerve holds use grabbing, pressing, squeezing, and gouging actions to attack sensitive nerves or pressure points. Nerve holds are often used with, or are a part of, joint lock holds or chokes. They are used to cause pain, control movement, impair motor functions, reduce Ki-flow (weakening an attacker), or produce unconsciousness. The effect depends upon the point targeted, the degree of accuracy, and other combative principles outlined in the author's books, *Essential Anatomy for Healing and Martial Arts* and *Hapkido: Traditions, Philosophy, Technique*. These books also contain detailed anatomical drawings and descriptions outlining the precise locations of hundreds of pressure points and nerves.

Some of the more common nerve holds are shown at right. Many of these techniques can be used to assist throws, or initiate escapes from simple restraining holds and joint locks.

1. Hair Pull Hold

Pulling hair causes pain initially, although the level of pain diminishes with time. Hair pulling is mostly used to control head movement and to assist chokes and throws.

2. Hair-Knuckle Hold

Grab the hair and lever your knuckles into cranial nerves. Gallbladder and Bladder pressure points are common sites used to control movement or set up other techniques. The example at right shows an attack to GB-4, GB-5, GB-6, GB-7, and ST-8. These pressure points lie close together in a line, on a branch of the auriculotemporal nerve (ST-8 also intersects the temporal branch of the facial nerve).

3. Lip Hold

Grab the lip using your thumb and index finger. Pull, pinch, or twist to produce pain.

4. Double Lip Hold

Hook your index fingers into the corners of the mouth and pull them apart. This is very painful, since it forces the lips to stretch beyond their normal limits. Be very careful to avoid being bitten, since serious diseases can be transmitted through body fluids.

5. Mouth Hold

Grip the chin at both ST-4 pressure points with your thumb and index finger (the middle finger also works well). This hold is usually used to release a body hold or set up a throw. Other pressure points can be added by using your remaining fingers. Typical additional points include ST-2, ST-3, and ST-9.

6. Ear Hold

Grab one or both ears using your thumb and index finger. Pull, pinch, or twist to produce pain and control movement. There are about 180 pin-sized pressure points on the surface of the auricle, which are used in Eastern medicine to affect different parts of the body.

7. Clavicle Hold

Gouge your fingertips downward, into the recess behind the clavicle. Pull back toward the collarbone. This is the site of the brachial plexus, a major nerve network, and ST-12. This hold is often used to force an attacker to their knees, or assist a throwing technique. At the same time, you can also press your knuckles into the neck at ST-9 or ST-10.

8. Armpit Hold

This is the site where the cords of the brachial plexus divide into the major nerves supplying the arm. Clamp onto the head of the Pectoralis muscle, gouging your fingers deep into the center of the armpit. The HT-1 pressure point is located here.

9. Biceps Hold

Grip the biceps brachii muscle from either side and pinch inward with your fingertips between the muscle and bone.

10. Inner-Elbow Hold

Grip and gouge the inner elbow, pressing two sensitive pressure points with your thumb and middle finger. The points you grab will depend upon circumstances and orientation. LU-5, HT-3, PC-3, and LI-11 are common targets.

This hold is usually a component part of other holds or throws, as seen in the Bent-Wrist Hammer Lock shown in the *Shoulder Locks* chapter. It can also be used to release a hold.

11. Testicle Hold

This hold is as painful as it sounds. Clamp the testicles using all five fingers. Gouge and squeeze, clashing them together.

12. Ankle Hold

Grip the ankle and press your inner index finger base joint (located on palm) into SP-6. This pressure point is located just above the protruding bone of the inner ankle, on the rear edge of the tibia bone. This is the site of the medial crural cutaneous nerve and the tibial nerve (deeper). If you are accurate, it is very painful. The surrounding area is usually less sensitive, depending on the person. This hold is used to force a fall, control the leg, or to release arm bars or chokes applied with the legs during ground fighting. The photo shows a throw from a seated position.

1. Hair-Pull Hold

2. Hair-Knuckle Hold (gouge cranial nerves)

3. Lip Hold (pinch and twist)

4. Double Lip Hold (pull apart)

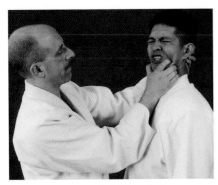

5.1 Mouth Hold (gouge both ST-4 points)

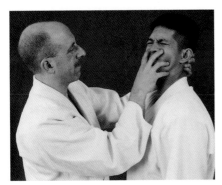

5.2 Mouth Hold (gouging ST-2, ST-4, ST-9, ST-10)

6. Ear Hold

7. Clavicle Hold

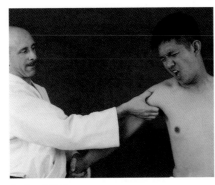

8. Armpit Hold

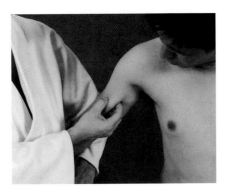

9. Biceps Hold

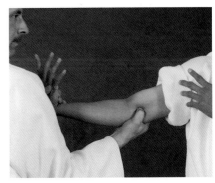

10. Inner-Elbow Hold

11. Testicle Hold

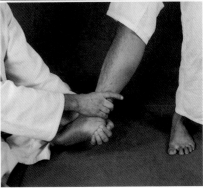

12. Ankle Hold (SP-6)

Real combat is rarely decided on the basis of a single technique. The ability to execute combinations of techniques and make transitions from one technique to another is crucial, as is the ability to recognize these opportunities during the flow of combat, which is constantly changing. For every technique, there is a counter; and for every counter, another counter. The more skillful your opponents are, the more easily they will move to negate your attack or defense. Holds can fail for any number of reasons, such as: your technique

COMBINATIONS

is insufficient, your opponent counters, or the dynamics of a situation change as you enter and the hold is no longer feasible. For this reason, it is important to develop skills that allow you to intuitively apply combinations and transitions as needed. Since this is a book about the art of holding, most combinations in this chapter will involve holds linked to holds, and occasionally, holds linked to throws. Naturally, holds can also be linked to strikes, kicks, chokes, pins, or any other technique that is appropriate.

BASIC CONCEPTS

When two or more techniques are linked together, they are commonly referred to as a "combination" or "transition." In the martial arts, both terms usually denote the same thing and are interchangeable, although some martial artists prefer one term over the other. Generally, combinations are used to:

- increase your chances of success, by using your first technique to setup subsequent techniques.

- provide a means of transition when the first technique fails.

Setting Up Techniques

One method of increasing your chances of success is to use the first hold as a feint to set up the second technique. In this scenario, the first hold either provides a distraction, generates confusion, or causes a reaction, any of which sets up your second technique. For example, you might fake a hold that unbalances your opponent to their rear. As they react defensively by leaning forward, you will quickly apply a second hold that unbalances them to their front, capitalizing on their initial reactions. The degree to which you commit yourself to the first hold depends upon your tactics and the situation. Your initial entry might involve very light body contact or a slight pull, or could involve more forceful contact and a pronounced effort to execute the hold, before shifting to the second technique. Against more skillful or athletic opponents, using combinations and feints is very important, since they create an opening for a particular technique that might otherwise be blocked or countered.

To be successful, a feint (the first hold) must deceive your opponent, causing them to misinterpret the situation. Virtually all skilled fighters make use of feints and are adept at recognizing them in their opponents. For this reason, successful feinting has a strong psychological component, in that you are attempting to predict and influence your opponent's responses to perceived attacks

or opportunities, without them knowing it. Effective feinting can be compared to skilled acting. If your feint is not convincing, your opponent will recognize it for *what it is*, instead of *what it is not*.

When the First Technique Fails

Holds can fail for a variety of reasons, such as: you make a mistake, your technique is poor, your opponent is too large or small for the hold you are attempting, your opponent moves to block your entry, your opponent resists with superior strength, your opponent avoids the technique, or your opponent begins a counter-technique or an escape.

When executing a hold, always be ready to make a transition at any time into other throws, strikes, or holds as circumstances dictate. When making a transition between techniques, try to capitalize on your opponent's actions and movements, and maintain pressure and control throughout the change. The hallmark of any masterful martial artist is that person's ability to make smooth, effortless transitions from one technique to another, constantly adjusting to the opponent's rhythm, balance, and power. If you are truly in sync with your opponent's movements, transitions should require very little effort. Sensitivity, feeling, and economy of motion are the most important qualities to cultivate. Strength is mostly irrelevant.

If you are confronting an opponent who negates your counters and transitions with superior skill or power, try switching your attack to a totally different part of the body. If an opponent's attention is focused on protecting the joints of one arm, then they will likely be unprepared for an attack to another area, such as the head, legs, or other arm. The key to successful transitions is to anticipate, and to move just slightly ahead of your opponent. When your opponent gets ahead of you, you will be vulnerable to counters. When you are *being controlled* by skilled transition artists, accelerate your movements ahead of theirs. This will provide the space you need to apply a counter and seize the advantage.

Power vs Blending

There are two basic conceptual approaches to applying combinations; they are characterized by the manner in which the second technique is applied. The first approach is to overcome your opponent's resistance to the first technique, by shifting to a second technique that employs greater force in the same direction (see page 168). The second approach is to overcome your opponent's resistance to the first technique, by using their own energy against them—commonly called *blending* (see page 174).

This first approach (greater force) tends to become less effective as your opponent increases in size or strength. However, it works well against similarly sized or smaller opponents, which is why it is used extensively in sport martial arts in which contests occur within weight classes. In this approach, the second technique is often characterized by using your entire body to generate force, and frequently involves dropping to the ground. Unfortunately, using greater force often leads to serious injuries when applying joint locks.

The second approach (blending) is more effective against larger, more powerful opponents, but requires greater skill and sensitivity to apply successfully. This approach tends to be emphasized in soft-styles or self-defense oriented martial arts, in which the size of your attacker can vary widely. Since the techniques in this book stem from Hapkido, the emphasis is on self-defense, and techniques that use blending and redirecting to make a combination work.

In reality, combination holds can incorporate both *power* and *blending* qualities. Thus, there really are not two distinct approaches, but rather an infinite number based on how these concepts become integrated into your combinations. The following pages show 20 typical combinations composed mostly of holds covered in earlier chapters. A great many other possibilities exist, some of which are outlined at right. Many of these combinations can also be applied in reverse order.

This chart lists typical combinations. The bold text is the first technique. The listings below each bold entry are different options for the second technique. Page number references are given after each technique. (*) An asterisk indicates the technique is shown in the author's companion book, The Art of Throwing.

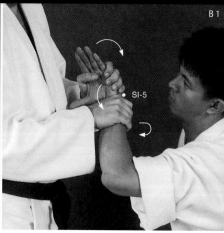

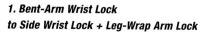
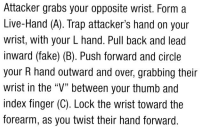

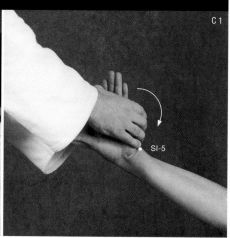

1. Bent-Arm Wrist Lock
to Side Wrist Lock + Leg-Wrap Arm Lock

Attacker grabs your opposite wrist. Form a Live-Hand (A). Trap attacker's hand on your wrist, with your L hand. Pull back and lead inward (fake) (B). Push forward and circle your R hand outward and over, grabbing their wrist in the "V" between your thumb and index finger (C). Lock the wrist toward the forearm, as you twist their hand forward.

To make a transition to a Side Wrist Lock, step backward and pull attacker's arm straight (D). Pull inward at their wrist with your little fingers, as you press the edge of their hand forward, toward the edge of their forearm, locking their wrist. A two-hand grip provides a more secure hold and better control. As the attacker drops to their knees (E), step in, swing your L leg over their arm, and lock their elbow with your inner knee (F). This transition can be used if an opponent resists your initial hold or straightens their wrist or arm, or you must move backward for any reason (e.g., avoid strikes, move attacker to a different location).

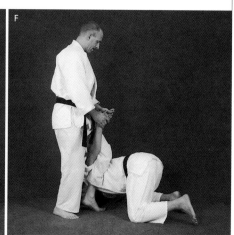

2. Bent-Arm Wrist Lock
to Forearm Arm Bar

Attacker grips your wrist with both hands. Form a Live-Hand (A). Use your free hand to trap their R hand on your wrist. Circle your elbow up, over, and down into their forearm to break their hold, as you deliver a Head Butt to the nose or eye (B), or a Shoulder Butt to the chest. Circle your held-hand up and over their wrist (C). Lock their bent-wrist by twisting their hand forward as you pull their wrist down toward your body (C1).

To make a transition to a Forearm Arm Bar, grip attacker's wrist, as you pivot both feet. Twist their wrist, pushing forward and down. Drive their bent-elbow up with your Live-Hand wrist (D). Step past attacker with your L foot and pivot 180° or more (E). Drive their elbow forward and down, as you pull their wrist outward and up, to straighten their arm and lock their elbow (F). Drop to one knee and pin. This transition can be used if an opponent counters the first hold either by: lifting their elbow; straightening their arm; or stepping away. If you are unable to pull their arm straight during E, shift to a Driving Shoulder Lock instead.

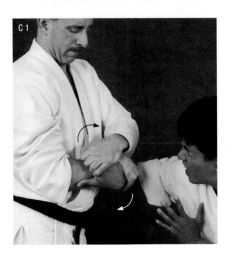

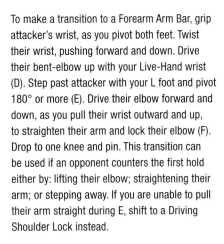

TW-11

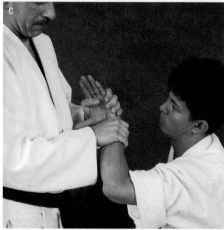

3. Bent-Arm Wrist Lock
to Outward Wrist Lock

Attacker grabs your opposite wrist. Form a Live-Hand. Trap attacker's hand on your wrist, with your L hand. Pull back and lead inward (fake) (A). Push forward and circle your R hand outward and over, grabbing their wrist in the "V" between your thumb and index finger (B). Lock the wrist toward the forearm, as you twist their hand forward.

If an opponent drops their elbow and twists their hand in the opposite direction, to counter your hold, make a transition to an Outward Wrist Lock: Maintain your hold at the wrist. Keep your other palm pressed tightly against the back of attacker's hand as they turn it outward (D). When their hand reaches the proper position, press down and twist their wrist outward (E), forcing them to drop (F). When rotating attacker's hand, the center of your palm pivots against their knuckles throughout the transition. Apply continuous pressure, keeping the wrist fully bent at all times. To perfect this motion, alternate back and forth, continuously, between both locks.

4. Outward Wrist Lock
to Knee Arm Bar Pin

Fade back as you parry a lead straight punch, from outside, using your R hand (A). Deflect the blow toward your L hand. Grip the wrist and fist with both hands. Based on attacker's actions, either step backward with your R foot or forward with your L foot. As you step, abruptly turn attacker's hand outward and down to your right, to lock their wrist (B), forcing a fall (C). After attacker falls, lock their elbow on your lower leg (D). Pull their wrist horizontally, forcing them to turn onto their belly. Kneel on their elbow at TW-11 and lock their wrist (E–F).

This transition can be used after any takedown or throw in which your opponent lands on their back in the same relative position as this example. In some cases, an opponent may not know that they need to roll over to keep their arm from being broken. If they need help, tell them where to go ("roll over on your belly please"), or grip behind their collar with your R hand and lift as you lever their arm. Once their shoulder lifts off the ground, the arm bar will accelerate their motion very quickly.

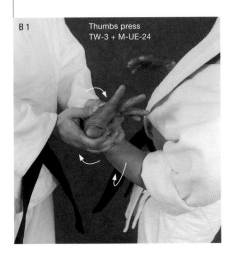

B 1 Thumbs press
TW-3 + M-UE-24

F 1

TW-11

5. Outward Wrist Lock
to Two-Finger Lock (pinky fulcrum)

Fade back as you parry a lead straight punch from outside, using your L hand (A). Deflect the blow toward your R hand. Grip the wrist and fist with both hands. Either step backward with your L foot or forward with your R foot. As you step, abruptly turn attacker's hand outward and down to your left, to lock their wrist (B), forcing a fall (C). As they fall, shift your grip and wrap the two smallest fingers. Force attacker to rollover by locking their fingers toward the back of their hand, using your pinky as a fulcrum (D). Do not pull their arm; they will roll over naturally. Step sideways and guide their elbow to the floor, as you continue locking their fingers and wrist (E). They cannot move without increasing pain.

If you wish to bring an opponent to their feet and escort them somewhere, rotate your hand counterclockwise until their palm faces upward. Continue locking their fingers, forcing them to stand up. If needed, you can force them to drop to the ground again by rotating their palm downward.

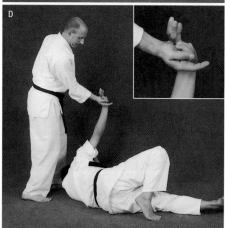

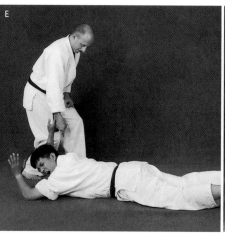

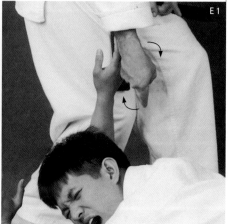

6. Elevated Wrist Lock
to Gooseneck Lock

Attacker grabs your cross wrist. Grip their wrist with your R hand (underhand), and grip their hand with your L hand. Step back with your R foot and pull their wrist to your hip (A). Step forward with your R foot, twist their wrist inward, and elevate their elbow (B). Pass under their arm, pivot 180°, and lock their wrist (C). Your fingers pull at the edge of their palm, and your thumb presses LI-4 at the web of the thumb. Keep attacker on their toes, stepping in a circle (D).

If an opponent attempts to counter by dropping their elbow and turning their hand outward (the hold turns it inward), transition to a Gooseneck Lock: As attacker drops their elbow, step close and trap their elbow between your arm and body (E). Maintain a two-hand grip on the hand, but allow it to shift slightly, so your fingers wrap the back of their hand, with your thumbs at their wrist. Lock their wrist by pressing their palm down toward their forearm (F).

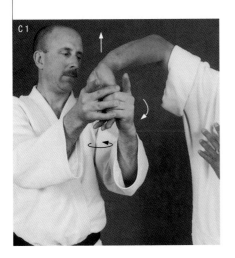

C

B

A

D

7. Gooseneck Lock
to Inner-Elbow Arm Bar
to Inside Shoulder Throw

Attacker grabs your opposite wrist. Form a
Live-Hand (A). Grab attacker's wrist with your
held-hand, as you chop their inner elbow with
your Ridge Hand (B), forcing the arm to bend.
Begin locking their wrist with one hand, as
your other hand hooks their elbow, pulling it
into your arm-body trap (C). Wrap the back
of attacker's hand with two hands (thumbs at
their wrist). Lock their wrist forward, pressing
their palm toward their forearm (D).

*Note: This transition can
also be used to enter an
Inside Twisting Arm Lock,
instead of an Inside
Shoulder Throw. This
transition is shown under
Basic Principles in the
Fundamentals chapter.*

E

If an attacker counters by straightening their
arm, pull their wrist to your R hip as you lock
their elbow by turning your torso horizontally
downward to your right (E–F). If an attacker
counters again by circling around you (ahead
of your hold), pivot to your left, in the opposite
direction (G). Pull their arm over your R
shoulder and wrap their upper arm with your
R arm, as you cross-step behind your R foot
with your L foot and pivot. Plant your hips on
their R thigh (H). Raise your hips as you bend
forward and pull them over your shoulder (I).

I

F

G

H

8. Front Wrist Lock
to Inside Twisting Arm Lock

From a relaxed stance (A), step 45° forward to your right, with your R foot. Grab opponent's L hand with both hands, placing your thumbs on the back of their hand at TW-3 and M-UE-24 (B). Pull downward (fake), then push straight upward, bending their hand forward to lock their wrist. Their elbow is pointing straight up and their forearm is vertical (C). This hold can be used to restrain an attacker while they are standing.

If you wish to force a fall, or attacker counters by straightening their wrist or turning their hand to the outside, transition to an Inside Twisting Arm Lock: Step under attacker's arm with your L foot and pivot 180°. At the same time, twist their wrist as you straighten it, locking the arm and shoulder (D). Continue to twist as you whip their arm forward and downward (E), to force a fall or dislocation. A skilled opponent will initiate a Flip Side Fall to save their arm (F). You can also use this entry (C–D) to shift to an Elevated Wrist Lock (see combination 6), instead of an arm lock.

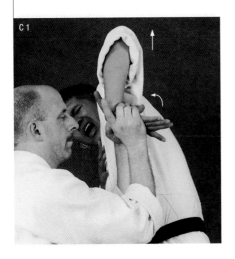

9. Scoop Palm Lock to Finger Hammer Lock

Attacker pushes you with one hand. Step back and absorb the push (A). Step 45° forward with your L foot. Pin attacker's fingers on your chest, with your L hand. Grip their elbow with your R hand (thumb at HT-3 or PC-3) (B) and scoop it upward and back toward you (C). This bends the fingers and wrist backward, stretching tendons and locking joints (C).

To make a transition to a Finger Hammer Lock, wrap attacker's index and middle fingers with your smallest finger on the base joints. Lock their fingers backward by pulling with your smallest fingers and pushing with your palm. Step under their arm with your R foot and pivot 180°, as you lever and twist their fingers (D). Place attacker's arm behind their back. Drive their elbow inward and back to lock the shoulder (E). Note that the shoulder is partially locked by step D.

Transitions to Chicken Wing Locks
Option 1: You can use this entry (A–D) to shift to a Chicken Wing Lock, by guiding attacker's arm to their side (F1), rather than behind their back. Grip the fingers, not the palm.
Option 2: If you reverse the roles of your hands when applying the Scoop Shoulder Lock (C), you can enter a Chicken Wing Lock (F1) without stepping under the arm.
Option 3: After step E, you can shift to a one-hand hold; like technique 10 (see D1), except the hand is locked as shown in F1.
Option 4: From step C, you can enter a Chicken Wing without stepping under the arm, by turning the fingers downward (F2).

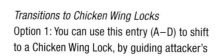
F 1   Chicken Wing Lock – Fingers Up

F 2   Chicken Wing Lock – Fingers Down

B

B

C

10. Straight-Arm Wrist Lock
to Gooseneck Hammer Lock

Attacker grabs your opposite wrist. Trap their hand on your wrist with your L hand. Lead inward (fake). Circle your R hand outward and up, as you step laterally and pull their arm straight (A). Lock their wrist forward as you twist their hand counterclockwise (B). This forces them to bend over to relieve pain. Sometimes an attacker will bend their arm and/or turn their back toward you to counter or relieve pain. If you continue to twist their hand, you will lead their arm behind their back. At this point, you can lock their shoulder by shifting to a Bent-Wrist Hammer Lock (see *Shoulder Locks* chapter), or a Gooseneck Hammer Lock as described next.

Transition to Gooseneck Hammer Lock (C–G)
This is a one-hand hold. Keep attacker's wrist and shoulder locked, as you trap their elbow between your inner elbow and body (C). Slip your L hand behind their arm and wrap the back of their hand, to maintain the wrist lock (D1). Reach around with your free hand and apply a Rear Lapel Choke (D–E). Unbalance attacker backward to prevent counters. If needed, thrust the blade of your foot into the back of their knee, forcing them to sit (F–G).

Transition to Gooseneck Lock (H)
From a Straight-Arm Wrist Lock (B), you can also shift to a Gooseneck Lock, by guiding attacker's arm to their side, instead of behind their back. Trap opponent's bent-elbow between your arm and body. Lock their wrist by pressing their palm toward their forearm, as you twist their hand outward (H).

D

E

H   Gooseneck Lock – Fingers Up

G

F

D 1

167

11. Elbow Arm Bar
to Rising Heel Kick + Armpit Arm Bar

Attacker grabs your lapel. Trap their hand on your chest, with both hands: your L fingers grip the edge of their palm, your L thumb presses the base joint of their thumb, and your R hand grips their wrist (A). Step across, twist attacker's hand until their elbow points up (B). Lock their wrist by fully bending it as you twist it forward. Lock their elbow by driving your inner elbow down into the elbow joint, as you lift their wrist (C).

This transition is very destructive and must be justified by circumstances. Pivot to your left as you execute a Rising Heel Kick by thrusting your heel upward to the face, throat, or solar plexus (D). Withdraw your leg, swing it to your left, and drop straight down as you reapply the arm bar (E). This breaks the elbow and/or dislocates the shoulder. Shift the arm bar to your armpit and pin (F). Spread your legs and plant your weight on the shoulder. Make sure you lock the wrist, as this reduces the need for strength. You can also lock the shoulder by levering attacker's arm forward.

12. Forearm Arm Bar
to Outside-Lift Shoulder Lock

This transition is shown as a knife defense, but can be applied to most unarmed situations in which your first technique is a Forearm Arm Bar. Step outside as attacker delivers an outward stab or strike (A). Execute a block to the elbow at TW-11, using your L wrist or forearm. Grip their wrist with your R hand (B). Apply a Forearm Arm Bar by driving attacker's elbow forward and down, as you pull their wrist backward and up.

If an attacker counters your arm bar by bending their elbow or by circling around to face you (ahead of your hold), pivot to your left. Grip their elbow (gouging LU-5 and HT-3) and bend their arm, circling their hand toward their head (C). Step in with your R foot and pivot. Bend the wrist and lock it outward (D). Step behind your R foot with your L foot and pivot. Lock attacker's shoulder by lifting their elbow inward as you twist and push their hand downward (E). Force a fall, maintain the lock, and pin (F). This transition can also be used to apply an Outside-Lift Shoulder Lock.

13. Inside-Block Arm Bar to Drop Bent-Arm Lock

Step outside a lead straight strike. Execute a L Inside Block to the elbow at TW-11, as you trap attacker's wrist between your forearm and your upper arm and chest (A–B). This locks or breaks their elbow in a single action, without grabbing. To apply the arm bar, press their elbow downward with your forearm as you lift their wrist.

If the attacker's elbow becomes bent for any reason—e.g., they retract their punch, they drop their elbow—pivot your body to your left, without stepping. At the same time, strike down into the head of the biceps and inner elbow, with your R wrist. Push downward as you turn your wrist against the inner elbow (painful), trapping attacker's bent-arm on your chest (C). Pull them toward their rear-corner to throw. As they fall, grab the wrist. Pull the wrist upward and back toward your upper thigh, as you lock the elbow on your knee (D). This transition is very fast and does not require you to secure a grip, making it useful against fast strikers. Execute *quickly* and *forcefully*.

14. Inner-Elbow Arm Bar
to Passing Forearm Arm Bar

Attacker grabs your cross-wrist (A). Grab their wrist with your held-hand, and cross-step forward with your R foot. Pull their wrist to your R hip, as your R hand reaches under their arm and grabs your own hand to assist (B). Lock their elbow against your upper arm by turning your torso horizontally downward, as you step across in front of their legs.

If an attacker counters or escapes by circling around you ahead of your hold (C), pivot to your left, in the opposite direction (G). Step past attacker with your R foot, pass under their arm, and pivot 180° (D–E), as you drive your elbow into the ribs or solar plexus (F). This forces them to bend over, setting up the arm bar. Twist their arm. Lock their elbow by driving your wrist down into TW-11, as you lift their wrist (G). As you enter under attacker's arm, try to lock their wrist as you pivot (F1). Your abrupt change of direction between C and E must be done very quickly, in a single fluid motion, using *one step*.

15. Inverted Arm Bar
to Rear Push Throw

Attacker grabs your opposite wrist. Form a Live-Hand (A). Grab attacker's wrist with your L hand, step forward, and lever your R hand free, as you lock or break the elbow with your R upper arm (B). Circle your R hand over and around attacker's arm. Rake TW-11 with your thumb-knuckle as you wrap the arm and lock the elbow (C). If an attacker remains standing, the hold is less secure, since you can be struck with their free hand or kicked. For this reason, it is usually advisable to take them to the ground. The following transition can also be used if they counter by bending their arm.

To shift to a throw, thrust your forearm back into attacker's nose or throat as you pull back on their wrist, locking their elbow across your chest (D). For power, rotate your forearm 180° as you push their head: begin with your palm down, finish with your palm up (D–E). Throw attacker to their rear or left rear-corner by unbalancing them over your knee (F). Rotate your shoulders as you throw. This throw works even if you lose control of their L arm.

16. Scoop Shoulder Lock to Wrap-Block Arm Bar

Attacker delivers a hook punch with their arm bent. From inside the blow, block outward to their inner elbow or wrist, using a Knife Hand (A–B). Wrap and scoop attacker's bent-elbow inward and up, as you trap their wrist in your armpit (C). If attacker straightens their arm or reorients their elbow to counter your hold, wrap their elbow tightly, trapping their wrist against your back (D). Use your inner elbow or upper arm to apply lateral pressure to the elbow joint. Pivot to your left to lock the elbow (E). Redirect the arm bar downward by leaning your upper body forward as you maintain constant pressure. Force a fall to attacker's left front-corner. Drop to one knee and pin (F).

Transitions between these two holds, back and forth, are often needed when applying either of these holds. You must constantly adjust based on the position and orientation of the attacker's elbow. If the elbow is bent and pointing down, apply the shoulder lock. If the elbow is straight, apply the arm bar.

Scoop Shoulder Lock if uncountered

*Outside-Chop Shoulder Lock
if uncountered*

17. Outside-Chop Shoulder Lock to Forearm Arm Bar

Attacker delivers a high straight strike or descending strike (Hammer Fist shown). Step forward with your R foot. Execute a R Rising Block with your forearm to attacker's wrist (A–B). Chop their inner elbow with your L Ridge Hand or wrist, bending their arm (C). To apply the shoulder lock, you must push their wrist down with your R hand, as you lift their elbow with your L forearm. If attacker resists or counters by forcing their wrist forward or lifting their elbow outward, use their own energy against them.

Pivot to your right as you drive attacker's bent-elbow upward with your Live-Hand wrist (D). Step past attacker with your L foot, then sweep your R foot around, pivoting 270° (E). Drive their elbow forward and down, as you pull their wrist outward and up, to straighten their arm and lock their elbow (F). Pull attacker's arm toward their right front-corner to unbalance them and force a fall. Drop to your L knee and pin by maintaining your hold or kneeling on their elbow.

18. Four-Finger Lock (index fulcrum) to Passing Armpit Arm Bar

This transition can be applied in any situation in which you are able to apply a Four-Finger Lock (index fulcrum) to attacker's cross-hand. A defense against a joint lock is shown as an example. You could also grab their fingers during close-range grappling, or by attacking first, or by grabbing the fingers during an open hand strike (e.g., a Spear Hand to your eyes).

As attacker applies a Forearm Arm Bar, grip their fingers, pressing your extended index finger against the base joints (A). Twist their fingers and push up (their palm faces up), as you pivot left and pull your L hand free (B). This locks the fingers and is a finishing hold that can be used to restrain an attacker while standing. To transition to an arm bar, twist attacker's hand with both hands, step under their arm with your R foot, and pivot 180° (C). Twist their hand until their elbow points up. Place your arm over the elbow (D). Push down to lock it, as you lift the wrist. Bend and twist the wrist to lock it also. Step 45° forward with your R foot, drop to your L knee, and pin (E).

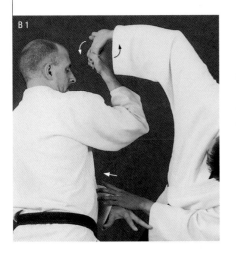

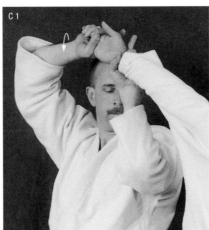

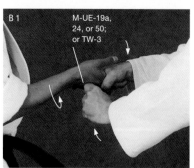

M-UE-19a, 24, or 50; or TW-3

19. Two-Finger Lock (rising) to Two-Finger Lock (dropping)

This transition shows how a finger lock is used to lead an attacker in different directions. From a false handshake (A), grip tightly and twist attacker's palm up, as you drive your index finger knuckle into the back of their hand at nerves between the metacarpal bones (B, B1). As attacker's grip loosens, slip your hand out and grip the two smallest fingers, pressing your index finger against the back of the base joints. Rotate your hand as you lever their fingertips toward their forearm. This forces attacker to tiptoe (C, C1). Use this hold to restrain them while standing, or pin as described next.

Maintain the finger lock as you turn attacker's hand so their fingers point toward their shoulder, with their palm facing up (D, D1). Continue levering their fingers and turn their palm laterally, forcing them to step and pivot in a circle and to pass under their own arm (E, E1). As they pass under their arm, turn their palm down and force them to their knees by continuing to apply the same lock (F). Keep your distance during this transition, to discourage counters. Always use the *finger lock* to control the rest of the body. This requires little effort when properly done (see *Finger Locks* chapter).

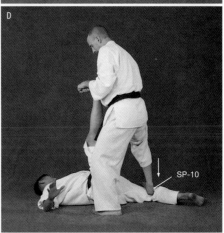

SP-10

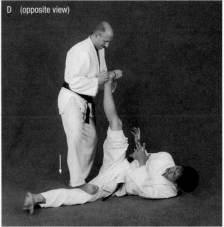

D (opposite view)

20. Twisting Leg Lock + Knee Pin
to Cross Leg Pin

This example shows a transition from one leg
lock to another. Steps A–D were covered in
detail in the *Leg Locks* chapter. Attacker pins
your arms from behind you, with one foot
forward. Thrust your Live-Hands forward and
buttocks backward, to break the hold and
unbalance attacker backward. Grip their ankle
with both hands (A). Pull up, locking the knee on
your buttock. Force a Back Fall (B). As attacker
falls, twist their foot outward with both hands.
Pivot 180° on your R foot and swing your L foot
into their head (C). Twist attacker's foot counterclockwise with both hands, as you pin their
knee by pressing your Knife Foot into SP-10 (D).

If you can't pin the knee or secure a strong leg-
twist: Twist the foot in the opposite direction, as
you press your knee sideways into the back of
attacker's knee, forcing them to turn onto their
belly (E). Keep their foot extended and pull it
toward you, pressing your shin into the calf at
BL-57 (F). Sit on their lower back, lean back,
and pull their foot. If they lift their free leg, grab
it and cross their ankles, pinning both legs (G).

G (opposite view)

F (opposite view)

E (opposite view)

Chokes and head locks are an important form of attack and defense used in many martial arts. Consequently, it is not only important to master the chokes and head locks themselves, but also common defenses against them. Because these holds are potentially very dangerous and life threatening, it is also important to be able to assess your opponents' skills to determine the degree of danger they pose. Even poorly skilled opponents, and individuals without martial training, are capable of inflicting serious injuries, most commonly,

DEFENSE AGAINST CHOKES + HEAD LOCKS

crushing the windpipe or breaking the neck. When learning defenses, you should first learn how to apply a specific hold before learning its counters. This will allow you to perceive the weak moments in your opponent's technique, and to understand the specific limitations of a given choke or head lock. Most comprehensive martial arts incorporating chokes and head locks also contain defenses against them. This chapter will present an overview of basic principles, and typical counters used in Hapkido and other martial arts.

BASIC CONCEPTS

The objective of most chokes is to force a submission, cause loss of consciousness, or effect death. In self-defense situations, forcing a submission is rarely the objective of your attacker. Consequently, *any choke* must be considered a serious threat, even if it appears incompetent. A choke that is loose and ineffectual could easily become life threatening in the span of a moment. A simple grip shift, or an adjustment in an attacker's technique, can make all the difference. Skilled martial artists will usually camouflage the specific choke they are working toward (you may not even be aware that they are maneuvering you into a choke). At the moment they obtain the best possible position, they will apply the choke suddenly and forcefully.

Once a strong choke is applied to the carotid artery, you will pass-out in 10–15 seconds. Since skilled vascular chokes are usually not painful, it can be very difficult to gauge the effectiveness of a choke being applied to you. As the blood supply to your brain is impeded, you will often become light-headed or dizzy just before losing consciousness. This might be the only warning you receive.

Chokes to the front of the windpipe are even more serious, since collapse of the trachea can block the air supply, resulting in death. This choke is not difficult to detect, and does not require the accuracy needed for carotid chokes. Coughing spasms and pain are present, even under light force.

Preventing the Entry

Your first line of defense is to prevent the hold from being applied, by countering during the entry or at the moment of gripping. The first two defenses shown on the next page employ this concept against a head lock from behind. Against a choke, simple Wedge Blocks or Spread Blocks can also be used to deflect the hands as they reach toward you, or at the moment your throat is grasped. You can also step out of range. If you are engaged in a grappling situation, the dynamics may be different: try to control the opponent's hands and arms to prevent them from securing the proper grip. Many times the best way to counter a choke is to apply one of your own.

Once the Choke is Applied

Any form of defense used against an applied choke must work quickly, before you are choked-out. Your first action when countering any choke is to break the hold, or at least reduce its effectiveness. Most chokes can be released by gouging your fingers into an attacker's eyes, throat (CO-22), or nerves at the elbow (TW-11, LU-5, HT-3, LI-11, SI-8).

To reduce a choke's effectiveness: drop your chin (tight to your chest), tense your neck muscles, and hunch your shoulders. This protects the windpipe and part of the carotid artery. The artery can still be pressed at SI-17 (side of the neck), although this is a much more difficult choke to apply. Tensing the neck and jaw will also increase your resistance to nerve attacks and prevent your head from

being jerked. This defense (drop chin, tense neck, hunch) works well against most chokes by inexperienced opponents. More experienced opponents will force an entry by using nerve attacks (see *Forced Entries* in *Chokes + Head Locks* chapter), or apply a choke by slipping their thumbs past the side of your chin to press ST-9 or ST-10. Since the side of the neck is hard to protect, nerve chokes to LI-18 or SI-16 are also possible.

If an attacker achieves a tight, clamping hold on your carotid artery, try to twist or move your neck in any direction. Even limited motion may loosen or shift the hold enough to allow blood to continue flowing. A reduced blood supply is better than no supply, and may be enough to keep you from losing consciousness. Biting the arm, or gouging the arm with your chin, are also useful. If your hands are free, execute forceful strikes to vital targets. Remember, any time an opponent chokes you with both hands, they cannot use them to block strikes. This is the vulnerable aspect of any two-handed choke.

Typical Techniques

Typical defenses are shown on the following pages, and are organized based on type of attack you are defending against: full nelson lock, front choke, front choke with the arms crossed, front naked choke, side choke, and rear naked choke. Many other defensive techniques exist, some of which can be found in the author's 1136-page book, *Hapkido: Traditions, Philosophy, Technique.*

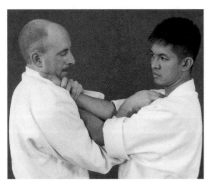

To release a choke hold: press into CO-22 (base of throat at suprasternal notch) as you step backward.

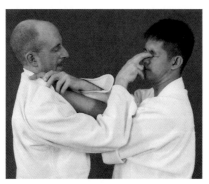

To release a choke hold: poke both eyes (lightly) as you step backward.

To reduce a choke's effectiveness: drop your chin, tense your neck, hunch, and pull the arm away.

DEFENSE AGAINST FULL NELSON

This head lock will break the neck if forcefully applied. Your first concern is always to relieve pressure and break the hold. Common methods of preventing the entry or releasing the hold are:

1. Block Entry: Pull your elbows to your hips. This prevents attacker's hands from joining, or breaks loose grips.

2. Drop Escape: Before the hold is tight, raise your arms overhead and drop straight down, slipping out of the hold.

3. Forehead Brace: Join your hands with fingers interlocked. Push back against your forehead to relieve pressure and prevent the hold from being applied.

4. Against Interlocked Fingers: Squeeze attacker's fingers together (very painful).

5. Against Lapped Fingers: Gouge nerves between tendons, and/or pinch cuticles.

6. Against Crossed Wrists: Grab one or more fingers. Bend back to lock joints.

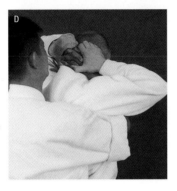
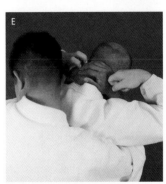
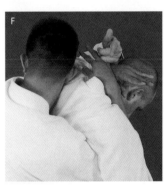

7. Poke, Stomp, and Finger Lock
Full Nelson (A). Poke the eyes with your fingertips, as you lift your leg (B). Stomp the toes. Press nerves at the back of the hand, with your index finger knuckle. As the hold loosens, peel back one or two fingers with your other hand (C). Lock the finger backward, step outside, and pivot 180° (D). Step back and force attacker to their belly (E). Many other finger locks are possible, based on which hand you grab with, and which fingers are held.

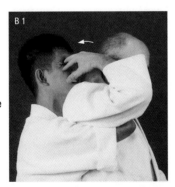
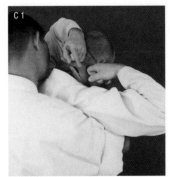
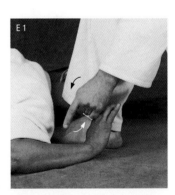

Ridge Hand

Inner Wrist

1. Against Front Choke

Use Bent-Arm Wrist Lock

Attacker chokes you with two hands (A). Step away, grip their cross-hand with one hand, and poke their throat using one or more fingers (B). Target CO-22, or ST-9 and ST-10. As the choke releases, twist their hand inward and hit their inner elbow with your L Ridge Hand or Inner Wrist (bends the wrist and elbow). Lock the wrist by rotating their hand toward their body midline. Pull the wrist down and back with the L hand (C–D), or shift to a one-hand grip (C2).

Important Points

This counter can be used against many types of front chokes (see *Chokes + Head Locks* chapter). If attacker drops their chin to protect their throat during step B, poke their eyes instead. If they straighten their arm, shift to a Side-Wrist Lock or an arm bar. When applying the Bent-Arm Wrist Lock (C), many other grips are also possible. Gripping the wrist overhand provides a stronger hold, but a slower entry (C1 is underhand). The one-hand hold (C2) is very strong, and leaves your other hand free to strike or block. Grip the fingers, not the hand.

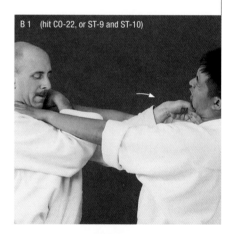

B 1 (hit CO-22, or ST-9 and ST-10)

C 1

SI-5

C 2 (one-hand hold)

2. Against Front Choke

Use Outward Wrist Lock

Attacker chokes you with two hands (A). Pivot 90°, grip their opposite-hand with one hand, and clamp the throat with the other, applying a Tiger Mouth Choke (B). All five fingers press nerves and arteries at ST-9, ST-10, and SI-17. Do not crush the windpipe. Choke as you twist the hand outward to lock the wrist (your thumb presses TW-3, your fingers pull the edge of the palm) (C). Pivot 180° and force a fall (D). Use a choke, arm bar, and wrist lock to pin attacker (E).

Important Points

This counter can be used against many types of front chokes (see *Chokes + Head Locks* chapter). If attacker drops the chin to protect their throat during step B, poke their eyes instead. Instead of clamping the throat, you can also poke it as shown in the previous technique, and then use both hands to apply the wrist lock. It is important to practice this counter along with the previous one, so that no matter which hand you grab, you will always have an option and react instinctively.

B 1 (clamp ST-9, ST-10, SI-17)

TW-3

C 1

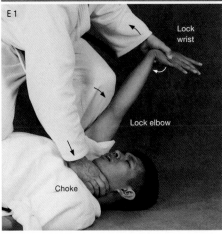

E 1

Lock wrist

Lock elbow

Choke

3. Against Front Choke (arms crossed)

Use Armpit Arm Bar

Attacker applies a Double Lapel Choke with their arms crossed (A). Pivot and hit their jaw with your elbow, as you grip the *top arm* (B). Your cross-hand grips their hand; your opposite-hand grips their wrist. Pivot in the opposite direction, twist their hand so the elbow points up, and lock their wrist (C). Lock their elbow by driving your armpit or upper arm down into joint, as you lift their wrist (D). Attacker's other arm is trapped by their own forearm and your forearm (C1). Maintain the hold as you drop to one knee and pin (E).

Important Points

Always grip attacker's top-arm on *top,* and turn initially toward its shoulder (B). Try to grip as far around their wrist as possible, so you will be able to rotate it fully, as you pivot in the opposite direction (C). As you apply the arm bar, try to clamp attacker's arm tight to your body, so their other arm is trapped. Lock their elbow with your armpit or upper arm. If their hand slips out, don't worry; maintain focus on the arm being locked.

E (side view)

B 1 (opposite view)

C 1

Trap

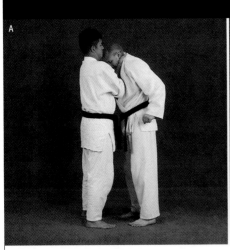

4. Against Front Choke (arms crossed)

Use Twisting Neck Lock

Attacker applies a Double Lapel Choke with their arms crossed, pulling you close to increase leverage (A). Deliver a Twin Uppercut Punch to the ribs at LV-13 (B), then a Twin Hook Punch to both temples at M-HN-9 (C). Grip the rear-corner of their skull with your L hand and plant your R palm on their chin (D). Twist the head to lock the neck, as you step forward with the R foot and pivot 180°, forcing a Side Fall (E–F). Apply force judiciously to avoid a broken neck.

Important Points

A skilled attacker will pull you in close to increase choke leverage. If they have proper grips, you can be choked unconscious very quickly. This counter uses a rapid series of devastating twin strikes to quickly break the choke. Modify your strike force based on the seriousness of the threat. Since you will hit the same pressure points on both sides of the attacker's body, the effect is magnified. You can also hit both sides of the neck at LI-18. When throwing, use restraint. To be gentle, reduce force and drop low to protect the neck.

C 1 (hit M-HN-9 or TW-23)

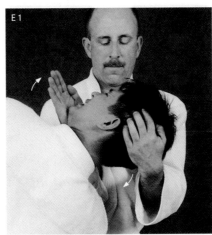

E 1

A (opposite view)

A 1

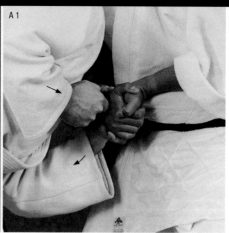

B

C

5. Against Front Naked Choke

Use Shoulder Lock + Arm Bar

Break the hold: pull attacker's arm downward with your L hand, as you press nerves on the back of their hand, with your index finger knuckle (A). As their hands unjoin, pull their *wrist* outward and upward with your L hand, as you lock it forward with your R hand. Pull their *bent-elbow* downward, lift your head backward, and lock their shoulder. Step under their arm with your R foot (B), and pivot 180°. Lock the elbow by pulling the triceps tendon down as you lift the wrist (C). Force a fall (D).

Important Points

Steps B–C show the quickest transition to an arm bar, without changing grips. Photo C2 shows a Two-Hand Arm Bar, which is a stronger hold, but uses grip changes (riskier): trap the hand on your R shoulder before pivoting, lock the elbow as you turn. Front Naked Chokes are very dangerous holds. If an attacker can achieve proper lift and leverage, they will create extreme stress along your cervical spine and crush your windpipe. Keep this in mind when selecting counters.

D

C 1

C 2 (alternate hold: see note top right)

A

B

C (concussion and Driving Shoulder Lock)

D

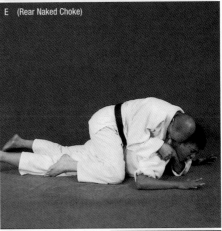

E (Rear Naked Choke)

6. Against Front Naked Choke

Use Concussion + Shoulder Lock

Relieve pressure: wedge your R forearm between attacker's elbow and armpit, and pull their wrist down with your L hand (A). Step close, lower your hips, lift your head, sit backward (B). Attacker will usually release one hand to prevent a concussion when falling. Wrap their waist with your legs. Lock or separate their shoulder by pushing their hips away from you as you lift their wrist and arch your head back (C). In one continuous motion, shift your hips to your left, so that you are no longer under attacker (D), then roll on top and apply a Rear Naked Choke (E).

Important Points

Sometimes the only way to break this choke is to go to the ground. This radically alters attacker's use of body weight and leverage, providing the opportunity to counter, as shown in this technique. If the attacker has a secure hold, and you drop back quickly and forcefully, you will likely cause a concussion as their head slams into the ground. At the very least, it will loosen their choke hold.

A 1

C 1

E 1

A (gouge hand)

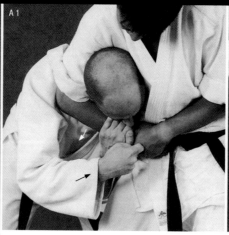

A1

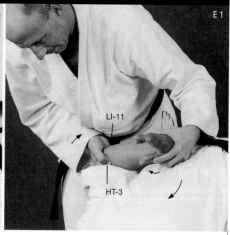

E1

LI-11

HT-3

B (stomp)

C (spear groin)

7. Against Side Choke

Use Three Strikes + Hammer Lock

Attacker wraps your neck from the side. Pull their arm down with your L hand. Hit or gouge nerves on the back of their hand using your knuckle(s) (A). Stomp their foot at LV-3 with the edge of your heel (B). Thrust your fingertips into their groin at LV-12 and SP-12 (C). These three blows can be used singly or combined, to unjoin the hands. As the hands part, pull the wrist back and push the elbow forward (D). Place attacker's bent-arm behind their back (E). Lock their wrist and shoulder by bending their wrist and lifting it toward their shoulder, as you push their elbow inward (E1). Force attacker to their belly. Pin them by kneeling on their neck, as you use your L leg and L hand to maintain the hammer lock (F).

Important Points

When entering, grip attacker's elbow at HT-3 and LI-11, pressing sensitive nerves. You can also grip LU-5 or SI-8. This entry (A–D) can also be used to apply an Elbow Hammer Lock, Elevated Wrist Lock, or a variety of different arm bars (see earlier chapters).

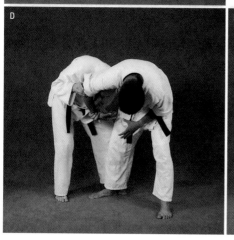

D

E

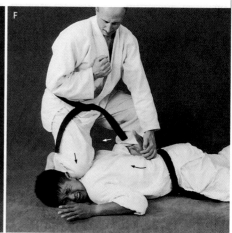

F

8. Against Side Choke

Use Clasped Bent Wrist Lock

Attacker applies an Arm Scissor Choke with their hands joined (A). Grip attacker's clasped hands with both of yours, clamping their hands tightly between your palms. Pivot low toward attacker as you twist their hands 180°, forcing their wrists to cross and your head to slip free (B). Lock the top wrist by rotating attacker's hands forward, toward their body midline (C). Drop to one knee. Pin by kneeling on attacker's arm as you lock their wrist (D).

Important Points

This is a variation on a basic Bent-Arm Wrist Lock. It is specifically designed to counter the formidable Arm Scissor Choke. If attacker interlocks their fingers when choking, you can also clash their fingers together as you twist their hands (very painful). When locking the wrist, use a tight circular motion (C1), focusing force at SI-5. Stay close, keep their arms bent, and use your body weight to assist the hold. When pinning, both arms are trapped. It is often possible to lock both wrists, combining a Bent-Arm Wrist Lock and Outward Wrist Lock.

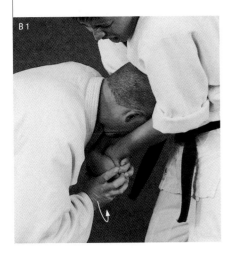

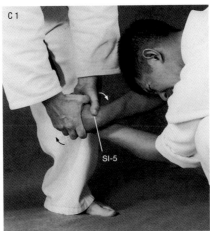

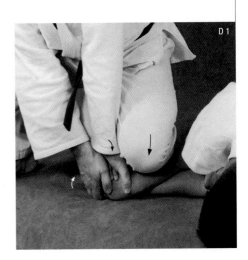

9. Against Rear Naked Choke

Use Drop Inside Shoulder Throw

Attacker applies a Rear Naked Choke from behind (A). Drop your chin to protect the throat. Reduce pressure by pulling their arm down with both hands, as you step back with the R foot, past their leg (B). Pull their arm down as you drop to one knee, blocking their foot with your inner knee (C). This keeps attacker from stepping around to counter. Bend deeply forward, pulling them over your shoulder (D–E). This throw is very effective.

Important Points

Although standing throws are an option, this throw is most powerful when dropping. This allows you to use your entire body weight to assist. Make sure you trap their leg as you drop, planting your buttocks on the lower leg. The bodies are locked tight together as you throw. Most errors result from excess space. Drive your head toward your L leg (E). If a strong attacker prevents you from bending forward, shift your body to their right side and redirect the throw in that direction.

D (side view)

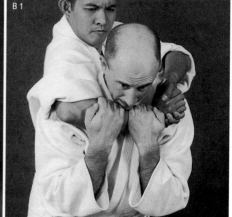

E (side view)

B 1

10. Against Rear Naked Choke

Use Elevated Wrist Lock

Attacker chokes you with one arm (A). Pull their wrist down with your L hand, lift their elbow with your R hand, and pivot 90° (B). Shift your grip to the hand and lock their wrist. Lock their shoulder as you duck under their arm (C). Twist their hand inward to lock their wrist. Keep them on tiptoes (D); or step forward, drop to one knee, pull downward, and throw. A skilled opponent will flip over to avoid injury (E). You can also shift to technique 7 by twisting and guiding attacker's arm behind their back.

Important Points

During steps B–C, you will change your wrist-grip by pivoting your palm on the back of attacker's hand. During the grip-shift, the side of your thumb presses down, while it pivots on the thumb-side of their wrist. This prevents escapes by keeping pressure on their arm until you regrip. Finish with your palm pressing the back of their hand to lock the wrist. Grip the elbow at HT-3 and LI-11, or LU-5 or SI-8. Note Live Hands (C1).

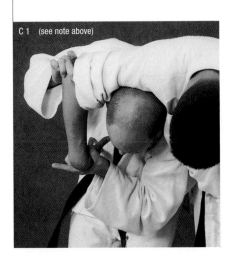

C 1   (see note above)

(grip with one or two hands)   D 1

Lock Pinky

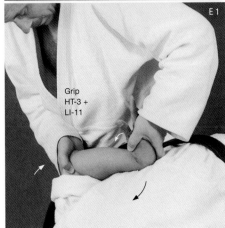

E 1

Grip HT-3 + LI-11

Joint lock holds are an important form of attack and defense found in many martial arts. Although these skills are primarily employed by mature martial artists for self-defense or sport, it is also possible that these same sophisticated techniques may be used to harm you. Consequently, it is not only important to master the holds themselves, but also common defenses against them. When learning joint lock defenses, it is crucial to first learn how to apply a specific lock before learning its counters. This will allow you to perceive the weak

DEFENSE AGAINST JOINT LOCKS

moments in your opponent's technique, and to intimately understand the specific limitations of a given hold. This in-depth knowledge also helps you to assess your opponent's skills, to determine the best course of action. Most comprehensive martial arts systems that incorporate joint locks also contain defenses against them, although this material is rarely taught or published. This chapter will present an overview of basic defensive principles, and typical countertechniques used in Hapkido, which are also used in other martial arts.

BASIC CONCEPTS

Proficiency in applying joint lock holds in combat situations takes years to master. Consequently, most joint lock attacks directed at you are likely to come from skilled opponents. Their level of skill determines the degree of danger they pose. Since most joint locks can cause serious damage—broken bones or torn muscles, tendons, and ligaments—your first concern is always to nullify the hold and protect your joints.

Before the Hold is Applied

The easiest way to avoid most joint locks is not to get in them. While this may seem self-evident, it is also a fairly realistic option. Since most joint locks cannot be applied unless they are unexpected or well set up, anticipation and prevention are the best defenses. The sooner you detect the attack, the easier it will be to counter. You can also avoid many joint locks by avoiding vulnerable situations. For example, don't fight or grapple with your arms straight, since you're inviting an arm bar; keep your fingers protected, or they will be grabbed and broken.

After the Hold is Applied

Against a novice, almost any form of counter will usually nullify a hold. Simple resistance or counterstrikes will often suffice. Against a more knowledgeable opponent, or one who is much stronger, more sophisticated techniques are required. Since most joint locks require a precise and skillful application of complex forces in order to work, a simple adjustment in your body position will often neutralize the hold. While this sounds easy, *where you move* makes all the difference. You must understand the inherent weaknesses in the hold you are countering—why it works and why it usually fails. This tells you where and how to move. Although the answers are very simple once you grasp them, they can take years of practice to attain. In a sense, these things cannot be taught; they must be felt.

For example, if an attacker is applying a Bent-Arm Wrist Lock to you (see example in *Wrist Locks* chapter), they must align your hand with the centerline of your body. If you can move your hand or change your body position slightly to alter this angle, you will probably neutralize the hold. Arm bars are easily negated by changing the position of your elbow. Only a very skilled practitioner will possess the sensitivity to counter or adjust to these slight changes.

Defensive Actions

When defending against attackers attempting to apply joint lock holds, there are several basic defensive concepts you should apply. Many of the counters shown in this section incorporate these actions.

1. Try to detect the attack at the earliest possible moment. Avoid the hold by stepping, or by changing your body position. For example, twisting or bending your arm will negate most arm bars. Keeping your wrists free from grabs will prevent an attacker from controlling your arms. If your wrists are grabbed, try to lever them free, or bat the attacker's hands away. One very simple and effective method of freeing your wrist is to circle your hand around the attacker's wrist in a tight 360° motion, in either direction, driving the blade of your hand into their wrist.

2. Counter or escape before the hold is tight. Once your joint is locked, counters are more difficult, if not impossible. If the hold is well applied, you may not even be able to move.

3. Move ahead of the attacker's motion, blending with their force. This creates slack in the hold, which is needed to set up a counter or an escape. If a hold is being used to throw, initiate a fall before the attacker is ready. This unexpected motion often creates an escape or unbalances your opponent.

4. Execute strikes to distract the attacker. Often they will be concentrating all their resources on applying the hold, and will be unprepared for attacks to other areas. Many martial artists operate under the misguided notion that their holds prevent them from being hit. This is rarely true. The eyes and throat are often vulnerable. Pressure points can be found throughout the body. Low kicks to the shin and kneecap are very effective.

5. Try to force the attacker to operate from a weak position (e.g., hands held high or away from their body). Keep them from using their body weight. Try to disrupt their balance by forcing them to take awkward steps. Pushing, pulling, or twisting as an attacker attempts to apply a hold will often cause it to fail and may create an opportunity for a counter.

6. When you cannot escape or counter, channel all your energy into resisting the hold. Focus your mind on a single task: resistance. Visualize your held limb moving in the opposite direction of the attacker's force. Use jerky motions to disrupt an attacker's force. Talking or yelling can also be disruptive. If you can tumble or drop to the ground, this often creates slack in the hold. Always try to keep moving, even if you don't know where you're going or what you're doing. *Anything* that causes your opponent to hesitate may provide the opening you need to save your joints and initiate an escape. Be ready to capitalize on any opening that appears.

Typical Techniques

Defenses Against Joint Locks are advanced techniques usually learned at the black-belt level, although there is no reason they cannot be learned sooner. However, before learning these techniques, you must first learn how to apply all the holds you will be defending against. Understanding the hold, allows you to perceive the weak moments in your opponent's technique, and to truly understand the mechanics of counters you must apply.

Ten typical counters are shown on the following pages. Since this is a book about *holding*, most of these techniques will involve counterholds. Naturally, counters to joint locks can also involve strikes or throws. For those seeking a more comprehensive selection of countertechniques, please reference the author's 1136-page book, *Hapkido: Traditions, Philosophy, Technique.*

Alter Position

Alter the position of your body or limbs, to negate leverage. For example, bend your arm and drop your elbow to negate most arm bars.

Blend with Force

Move ahead of an attacker's motion, to create slack in the joint lock. For example, execute a Forward Shoulder Roll to escape a Forearm Arm Bar.

Execute Strikes

Execute strikes to distract or discourage further attack. For example, kick to the knee or groin against an Elevated Wrist Lock.

Grab Fingers

Grab any fingers that are loose or exposed, and apply a Finger Lock. For example, grab and lock the fingers of a Live-Hand, to counter a Bent-Arm Wrist Lock.

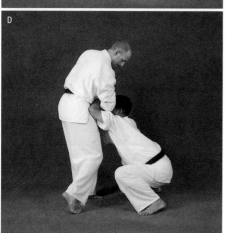

1. Against Bent-Arm Wrist Lock

Use Bent-Arm Wrist Lock

Attacker applies a Bent-Arm Wrist Lock. As the wrist lock is applied (A), reach across with your free L hand and grab the hand holding your wrist (B): your fingers grip the edge of the palm, your thumb presses LI-4 in the web of the thumb. Twist attacker's hand inward, as you rotate your R elbow over their forearm. Their wrist and elbow are bent about 90° (C). Lock attacker's wrist by twisting their hand forward, as you push your R arm downward into their forearm, pulling it toward you (D).

Important Points

In this counter, you will apply the same hold to your attacker that they apply to you. As you reach across, press your L arm downward into their arms (B1). This limits their wrist and arm movements, preventing them from fully applying the wrist lock. As you apply the counter, use your R arm to push downward and inward, keeping their wrist and arm close to your body (D). Maneuver your upper body over the hold, to assist leverage.

A

B

C

D

2. Against Outward Wrist Lock

Use Outward Wrist Lock

Attacker applies an Outward Wrist Lock (A). Use your free hand to grab their opposite hand and twist it outward: your thumb presses TW-3, your fingers pull the edge of the hand. Step 45° forward with your R foot and pivot, as you turn your held-hand downward, and lift your elbow inward (B). These three actions (stepping, turning your hand, lifting your elbow) relieve the pressure on your wrist (B1). Lever your hand free. Apply an Outward Wrist Lock with both hands (C), forcing a fall (D).

Important Points

In this counter, you will apply the same hold to your attacker, that they apply to you. The counter should be applied in one quick, fluid motion. Strength is not important; blending with attacker's force is. As you step and pivot, your hips should pass very close to attacker's hips. This reduces stress on your wrist and helps unbalance your opponent. When applying the wrist lock (C1), your thumbs press TW-3 and M-UE-24.

A 1

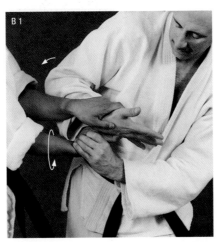

B 1

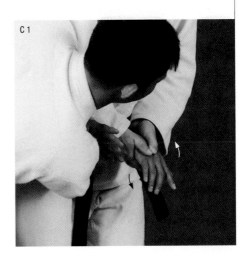

C 1

3. Against Elevated Wrist Lock
Use Armpit Arm Bar

Attacker locks your wrist, with one hand (A). Step across with your R foot and turn with the lock, creating slack in the hold. Grip attacker's wrist with your free hand (overhand grip) and twist their wrist, as you sweep your elbow forward (B). Collapse your wrist and drop your elbow over attacker's arm. Rotate your held-hand behind their hand (C1). Lock their elbow by pushing your armpit downward, as you lift their wrist (C). Swing your R leg to the side and drop downward (D), pinning attacker (E).

Important Points

There are many intricate, simultaneous motions that contribute to making this counter successful. They are all done quickly. As you drop your elbow (C), trap attacker's arm tight to your body, with your armpit on their elbow. Dropping quickly (D) will usually break their elbow or dislocate their shoulder. When using the arm bar to pin, spread your legs and plant weight on attacker's shoulder. Try to use a wrist lock to assist (E). You can also lock the shoulder by levering their arm forward.

A

B

C

D

E

4. Against Inverted Arm Bar

Use Scoop Shoulder Lock

As the arm bar is applied (A), slap up with your L palm into your R hand, bending your arm. At the same time, lower your hips, shift them sideways, and pivot 180° (B). Pivot another 180° as you step around with your R foot and pass under attacker's arm (C), pulling their elbow with you (D). Scoop their bent-elbow inward and upward, trapping their wrist in your armpit (E). Step backward and force a Back Fall (F). If necessary, you can block or sweep their L leg with your R foot.

Important Points

Apply this counter in one fast, continuous motion, using your 360° pivot to power the counterhold. When lifting attacker's bent-elbow, drive upward with your wrist, forearm, or thumb-knuckles. Use a Live-Hand for power (E1). This hold can be difficult to apply against taller people. If the hold fails, try lifting with two hands or adding strikes. If attacker extends their arm, make a transition to a Lapel-Assist Arm Bar or an Inner-Elbow Arm Bar (see *Arm Locks* chapter).

E1

F

5. Against Elbow Arm Bar

Use Turning Elbow Strike + Outer Reap

As attacker enters the arm bar (A): pivot 180°, bend your arm behind your back (B), and deliver an Outside Elbow Strike to the base of the skull at GB-20, BL-10, GV-15, or GV-16 (C). Sweep your arm past attacker's head, and wrap their neck. Plant your inner elbow on their throat, and lift their chin with your elbow (D). Throw by pulling their head downward as you sweep your leg backward into their calf. Reap their leg upward (E).

Important Points

When clamping attacker's neck, try to apply a choke, using your biceps and lower arm muscles (tensed), and the edge of your forearm. You will be pressing to both sides of their neck at the carotid artery (ST-9 and ST-10). Rather than choking, you can also hit into throat with your inner elbow or inner forearm, as you reap the leg. Try to grab their wrist (behind your back) and pull their arm as you throw. Drive your upper body forward and downward for power.

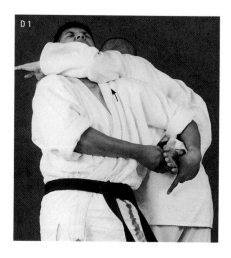

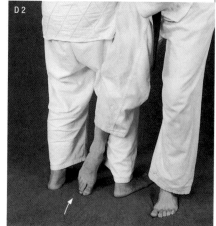

6. Against Forearm Arm Bar

Use Four-Finger Lock

As the arm bar is applied (A), grip attacker's fingers, pressing your extended index finger against attacker's base joints. Squeeze their fingers together, clashing the joints (B). Twist their hand 180° and push upward (palm up, elbow elevated). This neutralizes the arm bar (C). Rotate your hand as you lock their fingers toward their forearm (D). You can either force them up onto their toes and restrain them while standing, or take them to the ground. To pin, turn attacker's fingers until their palm faces down. Continue to lock their fingers, forcing them to the ground (E).

Important Points

Twisting attacker's hand and pushing up is crucial (C). This negates their arm bar and prevents them from reapplying another arm bar with their elbow or armpit. This entry can also be used to apply an Elevated Wrist Lock (see *Wrist Locks* chapter). When locking the fingers or turning the palm downward, use small, tight circular motions.

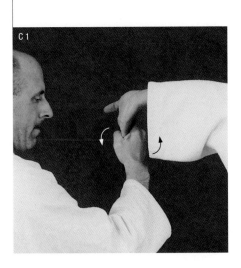

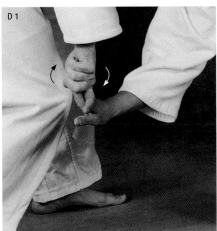

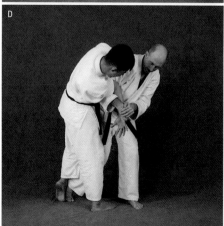

7. Against Front Shoulder Lock

Use Front Shoulder Lock

Attacker locks your shoulder, using both hands (A). Pivot toward them (relieves pressure) and execute a L Hook Punch to the back of the jaw at TW-17, then grip your R hand. Step in front of attacker with your R foot and pivot 90°. Pull your R arm forward to relieve pressure, locking attacker's shoulder (C). Pull their wrist downward with both hands, as you lift their elbow with your R elbow (D). Unbalance attacker toward their right side and force a fall. A skilled opponent will initiate a high Side Fall to avoid a dislocation (E).

Important Points

In this counter, you will apply the same hold to attacker that they are applying to you. The initial punch distracts and loosens their hold. Grabbing your own hand prevents the lock from being fully applied. Pull forcefully with both arms. The pivot (B–C) is important, since this redirects force unexpectedly sideways. Otherwise, you are pulling directly against attacker's force. Keep your hand in front of your shoulder to prevent counters.

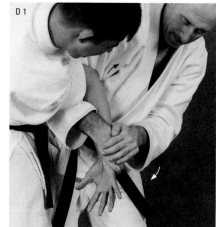

8. Against Scoop Shoulder Lock
Use Hand Sweep Throw

As attacker scoops your bent-elbow upward to lock your shoulder: step forward with your R foot (stay close), lower your body, and turn away to create slack in the hold (A). Raise your elbow (fully bent), pivot 180°, and drop to one knee (B). Pull attacker's upper arm forward and downward, as you thrust your L elbow into the back of their knee at BL-54 (C). Drop your L hand to their ankle (D) and sweep it upward, as you pull their arm downward, forcing a Back Fall to attacker's rear or left rear-corner (E–F).

Important Points

When scooping your elbow (A), attacker will be lifting and leaning their upper body slightly backward, as they apply the lock. You will attempt to capitalize on this natural motion, by unbalancing them backward. You must drop and pivot in a single, well-timed, continuous motion—before they can adjust. Pull the attacker's upper arm toward their rear or left rear-corner, as you sweep their leg. Your L arm traces a circular path.

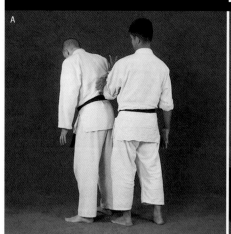

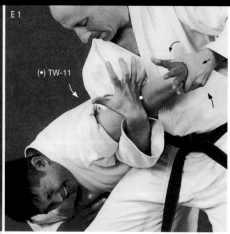

9. Against Elbow Hammer Lock
Use Passing Underhand Arm Bar
Attacker locks your shoulder (A). Create space
by thrusting your buttocks backward into their
waist (B). This unbalances them backward
and loosens the lock. Cross-step behind your
L leg, with your R foot. Pivot 180° and pass
under attacker's arm (C). As you exit, grab
their wrist and wrap your R arm under their
elbow (D). Lock attacker's elbow by pressing
the edge of your Live-Hand downward into
TW-11 (triceps tendon), as you lift their
locked-wrist (E). Unbalance them toward
their left front-corner, force a fall, and pin (F).

Important Points
The elbow can be locked using either edge of
your hand (E1, F). This hold is not as strong
as arm bars in which you wrap over the top;
however, it provides a quicker entry in this
situation. Be sure to *twist* attacker's hand
forward, as you *bend* it inward. This locks the
wrist (painful), turns the elbow up (for the arm
bar), and forces them to bend over. You can
also counter using a Straight-Arm Wrist Lock,
Elbow Arm Bar, or Forearm Arm Bar.

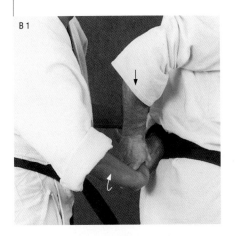

10. Against Bent-Wrist Hammer
Use Elevated Wrist Lock + Stomach Arm Bar
Attacker locks your wrist and shoulder (A). Reach back with your free hand and grip their L hand: your thumb pulls their little finger, as your fingers push their thumb. Twist their hand inward and push down. Straighten your locked wrist (B). Step backward under attacker's arm with your L foot (C). Twist their hand inward, locking the wrist and little finger (D). This is an Elevated Wrist Lock and is a finishing hold if desired.

Pull attacker's arm across your thighs and lock their elbow on your belly, as you punch the back of their jaw at TW-17 (just below the ear), using a Fore Fist (E). When punching TW-17, hit back-to-front. Use your smallest base-knuckle so you can pinpoint the pressure point (E1). If you wish to apply a choke, tightly wrap your L arm around attacker's neck, then press your wrist and forearm into the carotid artery or windpipe, as you continue to lock their elbow on your belly. Pull their wrist up and expand your belly (F).

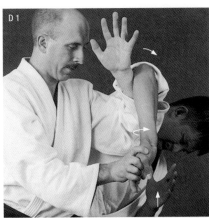

Punch TW-17

FURTHER READING

Philosophy and Religion

Chan, Wing-Tsit, trans. and comp.
A Source Book in Chinese Philosophy.
Princeton NJ: Princeton University Press, 1963.

Earhart, Byron H, edit.
Religious Traditions of the World.
San Francisco: HarperCollins Publishers, 1993.

Smith, Huston
The Illustrated World's Religions:
A Guide to Our Wisdom Traditions
San Francisco: HarperCollins Publishers, 1994.

Zimmer, Heinrich.
Philosophies of India.
Edited by Joseph Campbell.
Princeton NJ: Princeton University Press, 1969.

Medicine

Cohen, Kenneth S.
The Way of Qigong: The Art and Science
of Chinese Energy Healing.
New York: Ballantine Books, 1997.

Dox, Ida; John Melloni; and Gilbert Eisner.
The HarperCollins Illustrated Medical Dictionary.
New York: HarperCollins Publishers, 1993.

Kaptchuk, Ted J.
The Web That Has No Weaver:
Understanding Chinese Medicine.
New York: Congdon & Weed, 1983.

Maciocia, Giovanni.
The Foundations of Chinese Medicine.
London: Churchhill Livingston, 1989.

Netter, Frank H.
Atlas of Human Anatomy.
Summit, NJ: Novartis Pharmaceuticals, 1989.

Tedeschi, Marc.
Essential Anatomy for Healing and Martial Arts.
New York: Weatherhill, 2000.

Van Alphen, Jan, and Anthony Aris, editors.
Oriental Medicine: An Illustrated Guide
to the Asian Arts of Healing.
Boston: Shambala Publications, 1997.

General Martial Arts

Draeger, Donn F., and Robert W. Smith.
Comprehensive Asian Fighting Arts.
New York: Kodansha, 1980.

Farkas, Emil, and John Corcoran.
Martial Arts: Traditions, History, People.
New York: Smith Publications, 1983.

Haines, Bruce A.
Karate's History and Traditions.
Tokyo: Tuttle, 1968.

Nelson, Randy F., edit.
The Overlook Martial Arts Reader:
Classic Writings on Philosophy and Technique.
Woodstock NY: Overlook Press, 1989.

Tedeschi, Marc.
The Art of Throwing: Principles & Techniques.
New York: Weatherhill, 2001.
———. *The Art of Striking: Principles &*
Techniques. New York: Weatherhill, 2002.
———. *The Art of Ground Fighting: Principles &*
Techniques. New York: Weatherhill, 2002.

Periodicals

Aikido Journal. Tokyo, Japan.

Black Belt. Valencia, California.

Dragon Times. Thousand Oaks, California.

The Empty Vessel: A Journal of
Contemporary Taoism. Eugene, Oregon.

Inside Karate. Burbank, California.

Inside Kung Fu. Burbank, California.

Internal Martial Arts. Collegeville, Pennsylvania.

Journal of Asian Martial Arts. Erie, Pennsylvania.

Taekwondo Times. Bettendorf, Iowa.

Tai Chi and Alternative Health.
London, Great Britain.

Japanese Martial Arts

Draeger, Donn F.
Classical Budo.
New York: Weatherhill, 1996.

Funakoshi, Gichin.
Karate-Do: My Way of Life.
Tokyo: Kodansha, 1975.

Inokuma, Isao, and Nobuyuki Sato.
Best Judo.
Tokyo: Kodansha, 1979.

Kano, Jigoro.
Kodokan Judo.
Tokyo: Kodansha, 1986 (first published 1956).

Kudo, Kazuzo.
Dynamic Judo: Throwing Techniques.
Tokyo: Japan Publications Trading Co., 1967.
———. *Dynamic Judo: Grappling Techniques.*
Tokyo: Japan Publications Trading Co., 1967.

Omiya, Shiro
The Hidden Roots of Aikido:
Aiki Jujutsu Daitoryu.
Tokyo: Kodansha, 1998.

Otaki, Tadao, and Donn F. Draeger.
Judo: Formal Techniques.
Tokyo: Tuttle, 1983.

Pranin, Stanley.
Daito-ryu Aikijujutsu:
Conversations with Daito-ryu Masters.
New York: Aiki News, 1995.

Ueshiba, Kisshomaru.
Aikido.
New York: Japan Publications, 1963.
———. *The Spirit of Aikido.*
Tokyo: Kodansha, 1984.

Ueshiba, Morihei.
Budo: Teachings of the Founder of Aikido.
Tokyo: Kodansha, 1991 (first published 1938).

Tohei, Koichi.
Aikido: The Arts of Self Defense.
Tokyo: Ritugei Publishing House, 1960.

Chinese Martial Arts

Frantzis, Bruce Kumar.
The Power of Internal Martial Arts:
Combat Secrets of Ba Gua, Tai Chi, and Hsing-i.
Berkeley CA: North Atlantic Books, 1998.

Lee, Bruce.
Tao of Jeet Kune Do.
Santa Clarita, CA: Ohara Publications, 1975.

Yang, Jwing-Ming.
Taiji Chin Na: The Seizing Art of Taijiquan.
Boston MA: YMAA Publication Center, 1995.

Korean Martial Arts

Cho, Sihak H.
Korean Karate: Free Fighting Techniques.
Tokyo: Tuttle, 1968.

Chun, Richard, and P.H. Wilson.
Tae Kwon Do: The Korean Martial Art.
New York: Harper & Row, 1976.

Kimm, He-Young.
Hapkido 2.
Baton Rouge, LA: Andrew Jackson College
Press, 1994.
——. *Kuk Sool Korean Martial Arts.*
Baton Rouge, LA: Andrew Jackson College
Press, 1985.

Lee, Joo-Bang.
The Ancient Martial Art of Hwarangdo.
(three volumes)
Burbank CA: Ohara Publications, 1978.

Myung, Kwang-Sik, and Jong-Taek Kim.
Hapkido. (Korean language)
South Korea: 1967.

Suh, In Hyuk, and Jane Hallander.
The Fighting Weapons of Korean Martial Arts.
Burbank CA: Unique Publications, 1988.

Tedeschi, Marc.
Hapkido: Traditions, Philosophy, Technique.
New York: Weatherhill, 2000.

BOOKS BY MARC TEDESCHI

Hapkido: Traditions, Philosophy, Technique

Widely acclaimed the most comprehensive book ever written on a single martial art, this text contains over 2000 techniques encompassing all forms of martial skills: strikes, holds, throws, ground fighting, weapons, meditation, and healing. Also included are in-depth chapters on martial history, philosophy, and anatomy, plus interviews with 13 renowned martial artists. An authoritative presentation of basic principles and techniques, integrated with modern innovations, makes this work indispensible to martial artists of virtually any style.

1136 pages, 8 1/2 x 11 in.
Over 9000 b&w photos, maps, glossary, index
US $80.00 (hardcover), ISBN 0-8348-0444-1

Essential Anatomy For Healing and Martial Arts

This book familiarizes healing practitioners and martial artists with basic concepts of the human body, as defined by both Western and Eastern medical traditions. Written in a clear and concise style, this text presents material previously unavailable in any single text. Also includes principles of pressure point fighting, and 20 essential self-massage and revival techniques, along with detailed tables of acupoints in English, Chinese, Korean, and Japanese, cross-referenced to nerves, blood vessels, and other anatomical landmarks.

144 pages, 8 1/2 x 11 in., full-color
147 color drawings, 54 duotone photographs
US $19.95 (softcover), ISBN 0-8348-0443-3

Hapkido: An Introduction to the Art of Self-Defense

The first introductory text to accurately portray Hapkido in its entirety, this work is essential reading for anyone seeking a concise, accurate overview of Hapkido's history, philosophy, and techniques. Contains basic material to guide novices, plus more photographs and techniques than any similarly-priced competitive book. The first edition also includes a coupon for 20% off the 1136-page *Hapkido* (see above).

128 pages, 8 1/2 x 11 in.
680 b&w photographs, 48 illustrations
US $16.95 (softcover), ISBN 0-8348-0483-2

The Art of Throwing

This book outlines the core principles and techniques that define the art of throwing in most martial arts. An in-depth presentation of fundamentals is followed by over 130 practical throws, including shoulder throws, hip throws, leg throws, hand throws, sacrifice throws, combinations, and counterthrows.

208 pages, 8 1/2 x 11 in.
Over 1200 b&w photographs, 55 illustrations
US $29.95 (hardcover), ISBN 0-8348-0490-5

The Art of Striking

This book outlines the core principles and techniques that define the art of striking in most martial arts. An in-depth presentation of fundamentals is followed by over 400 practical strikes, including hand and elbow strikes, kicks, head butts, blocking and avoiding skills, combinations, and defenses against strikes and kicks.

208 pages, 8 1/2 x 11 in.
Over 1480 b&w photographs, 56 illustrations
US $29.95 (hardcover), ISBN 0-8348-0495-6

The Art of Ground Fighting

This book outlines the core principles and techniques that define the art of ground fighting in most martial arts. An in-depth presentation of fundamentals is followed by over 195 practical ground skills, including chokes, joint locks, pins, ground kicks, sacrifice techniques, and counters from seated, reclining, and kneeling positions.

208 pages, 8 1/2 x 11 in.
Over 1200 b&w photographs, 63 illustrations
US $29.95 (hardcover), ISBN 0-8348-0496-4

VIEW ONLINE
View samples or obtain information at:
www.tedeschi-media.com

HOW TO BUY
These books are available through retail book stores or direct from the publisher:

Weatherhill, Inc.
41 Monroe Turnpike, Trumbull CT 06611 USA
Sales: 800-437-7840; 203-459-5090
Fax: 800-557-5601; 203-459-5095
order@weatherhill.com

The Art of
HOLDING

Designed and illustrated by Marc Tedeschi.

Principal photography by Shelley Firth and Frank Deras.

Creative consultation by Michele Wetherbee.

Editorial supervision by Ray Furse and Thomas Tedeschi.

Production consultation by Bill Rose.

The following individuals appeared with the

author in the photographs: Arnold Dungo,

Cody Aguirre, and Jo-An Aguirre.

Also thanks to Merrill Jung for loaning

rare books from his personal collection.

The majority of the photographs were shot on

Plus-X Professional 2 $\frac{1}{4}$ film using Hasselblad cameras,

and were scanned from Ilford Multigrade prints

using an Epson ES-1200C flat-bed scanner.

Digital-type composition and page layout originated

on an Apple Macintosh 8500 computer.

Typeset in Helvetica Neue, Univers, Sabon,

Adobe Garamond, Weiss, and Times.

Printed and bound by Oceanic Graphic Printing

and C&C Offset Printing in China.

Published and distributed by Weatherhill.

Weatherhill

PUBLISHERS OF FINE BOOKS ON
ASIA AND THE PACIFIC